FROMMER'S

WALKING TOURS

Tokyo

P9-DCB-293

Beth Reiber

MACMILLAN • USA

ABOUT THE AUTHOR

Beth Reiber worked for several years in Tokyo as editor of the *Far East Traveler*. Now residing in Lawrence, Kansas, she continues to write travel articles and is the author of several Frommer guides: *Japan, Tokyo, Hong Kong, Berlin, Berlin from $50 a Day, Walking Tours: Berlin,* and *St. Louis & Kansas City.* She also contributes to *Europe from $50 a Day.*

MACMILLAN TRAVEL

A Simon & Schuster Macmillan Company
1633 Broadway
New York, NY 10019

ISBN 0-02-860466-0
ISSN 1081-3411

Editor: Theodore G. Stavrou
Map Editor: Douglas Stallings
Design by Amy Peppler Adams—designLab, Seattle
Digital cartography by Ortelius Design and
    Devorah Wilkenfeld

SPECIAL SALES

Bulk purchases (10+ copies) of Frommer's travel guides are available to corporations at special discounts. The Special Sales Department can produce custom editions to be used as premiums and/or for sales promotions to suit individual needs. Existing editions can be produced with custom cover imprints such as corporate logos. For more information write to: Special Sales, Simon & Schuster, 1230 Avenue of the Americas, New York, NY 10020.

Manufactured in the United States of America

CONTENTS

LIST OF MAPS

The Walking Tours

An Invitation to the Reader

In researching this book, I discovered many wonderful places—hotels, restaurants, shops, and more. I'm sure you'll find others. Please tell us about them, so we can share the information with your fellow travelers in upcoming editions. If you were disappointed with a recommendation, we'd love to know that, too. Please write to:

Beth Reiber
Frommer's Walking Tours: Tokyo
Macmillan Travel
1633 Broadway
New York, NY 10019

An Additional Note

Please be advised that travel information is subject to change at any time. The authors, editors, and publisher cannot be held responsible for the experiences of readers while traveling. Your safety is important to us, however, so we encourage you to stay alert and be aware of your surroundings. Keep a close eye on cameras, purses, and wallets, all favorite targets of thieves and pickpockets.

A Word About Japanese Symbols

Some of the establishments mentioned in this guide do not have signs showing their names in English letters. For those establishments, we have included the Japanese symbols next to the English transliteration.

INTRODUCING TOKYO

No matter how you arrive in Tokyo—by plane, bus, or train—there's no better introduction to the sprawling metropolis than the seemingly endless ride to the city center. Meticulously cultivated paddies, wooded hills, and tidy two-story homes gradually give way to factories, dusty parks, and concrete-banked rivers, until suddenly the open spaces vanish and you're in the midst of suburban Tokyo, with its crazy jumble of nondescript apartment complexes, residential neighborhoods, office buildings, department stores, mazes of overhead highways, and armies of people, all seemingly on top of each other and stretching as far as the eye can see. Tokyo's vastness is overwhelming, a bit numbing, and at first glance alarmingly monotonous. Without the ethnic diversity of many other metropolises around the world, the Tokyo ahead looks just like the Tokyo you left behind. Temples and shrines? Nowhere in sight. Traditional Japanese architecture? Swallowed by the concrete jungle.

Thus it is that first-time visitors to Tokyo are almost invariably disappointed. They come expecting an exotic Oriental city, but instead they find a metropolis Westernized to the point of drabness. Used to the grand edifices and monuments of Western cities, they look in vain for Tokyo's own monuments to its past. Indeed, from the looks of things, Tokyo's city plan is that there is no plan, with buildings erected haphazardly to fit whatever size plot is available, like weird pieces in a jigsaw

1

puzzle. To the uninitiated, Tokyo may well resemble a madman's vision of a massive penal colony, where the inmates have been sentenced to impossibly tiny cells, crowded commutes, intolerably long work hours, a strictly prescribed behavior, and limited leisure pursuits. No one with even the wildest stretch of imagination could call the city beautiful.

Tokyo's architectural nightmare may be attributed to two disastrous events that destroyed much of the city in this century—a 1923 earthquake that claimed 100,000 lives and leveled as much as 30 percent of the city, and 1945 bombing raids that laid half the city to waste. But the truth of the matter is that traditional Japanese architecture—constructed of wood—was never made to last, and judging from the vigor with which older buildings are torn down and replaced with taller and more lucrative ventures, Tokyo would look much as it does today even without the added incentive of tragic widespread destruction. After all, Tokyo's population has almost doubled since 1950, with 12 million people crowded into 800 square miles. Simply put, Tokyo is a crush of humanity, with land so scarce and valuable that most Tokyoites are forced to live on the never-ending outskirts, commuting to their jobs two to three hours a day on subways that are crowded beyond belief. In certain parts of the city at certain hours of the day, sidewalks are so congested that they could be described as bonafide human traffic jams. Go to a department store on a Sunday afternoon, and you'll swear that all of Tokyo is in there with you.

And yet, with all that said, I must confess that Tokyo is one of my favorite cities in the world, though it's an appreciation that came only with time. When I first moved here more than a decade ago, I was tormented with the unsettling feeling that I was somehow missing out on the "real" Tokyo, that it remained beyond my grasp, elusive, vague, and undefined. I was sure that the meaning of the city was out there somewhere, if only I knew where to look. But where to start? Tokyo has no city center, no central downtown, no beloved communal spot all Tokyoites call their own.

It was only after I started exploring different parts of the city that I realized Tokyo is best judged not by the sum of its parts but by the parts themselves. Although at first glance Tokyo may seem uninspiringly the same, upon closer scrutiny it reveals itself as a series of small towns and neighborhoods, merged together but each slightly unique in atmosphere, flavor, and history. Walk the quaint neighborhoods of Yanaka or Asakusa, for example, and you're worlds apart from the chic shopping district of Ginza. It's these neighborhoods of Tokyo that make the city both livable and lovable. And the more you roam, the more you'll discover of the city's gentler side.

Walk its streets, and you'll see mom-and-pop open-fronted shops, jam packed with everything from lacquered bowls to bright plastic buckets. You'll pass fruit stands with apples arranged like works of art, neighborhood tofu shops, and tiny neighborhood shrines nestled between high-rise office buildings. You'll walk down very narrow lanes, lined with carefully pruned bonsai and browse through shops selling beautifully crafted handmade goods. You'll find districts specializing in only one type of product, be it electronics or dolls, and, yes, you'll discover temples, shrines, and landscaped gardens, tucked away like jewels in the various neighborhoods. You'll even discover remnants of Tokyo's old downtown, in existence since the 1600s, in parts of Asakusa, Ueno, Yanaka, and points beyond, where there are still two-story wooden homes, narrow winding lanes, and centuries-old family businesses selling rice crackers, bean-paste buns, and traditional crafts. On the other side of the coin, Tokyo is also very hi-tech, a wonderland of exciting interiors. Innovatively designed restaurants, bars, and boutiques are a large part of what Tokyo is about—indeed, their number alone makes most other cities around the world seem boringly old-fashioned.

You'll also see things that will amuse you and even mystify you: Japanese bowing as they talk on the telephone; lots of vendors selling sunglasses in a nation where no one seems to wear them; vending machines selling cigarettes and even alcohol; apartment balconies that are never utilized in this crowded nation except for drying clothes; parking garages so small that they work like Ferris wheels; and rooftop beer gardens, shrines, playgrounds, and gardens. You'll see tiny mounds of salt outside restaurant doors, believed to ward off evil spirits; nighttime street stalls selling noodles, stewed vegetables, and alcohol; sidewalk fortune-tellers in nightlife areas such as Shinjuku and Shibuya; and employees in post offices and stores who still prefer the abacus to the calculator.

By walking Tokyo's streets, you'll also have more interaction with the Japanese themselves. On my very first day in

The Tours at a Glance

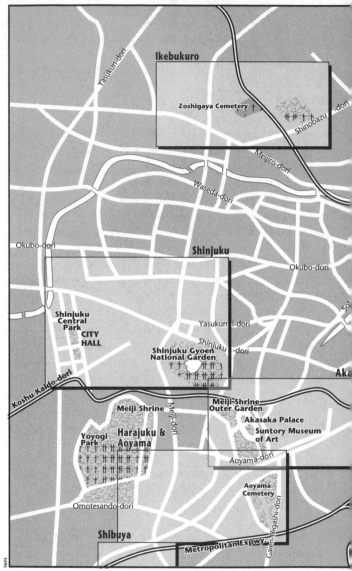

Japan, I was struggling with a large suitcase on a short walk to one of Tokyo's major train stations, oblivious to the light wet snow falling around me. Suddenly a young Japanese woman appeared at my side and held her umbrella over me, all the way to the station. She then whipped out a towel, dried my hair,

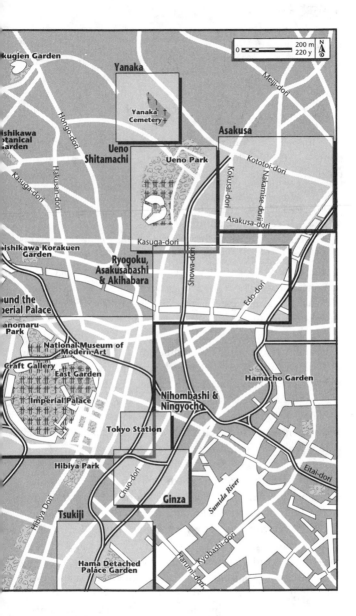

smiled, and disappeared into the crowd. I have had Japanese go miles out of their way to lead me to my destination. And there are few people on the face of the earth as honest and hardworking as the Japanese. They take pleasure in the task at hand, no matter how small or insignificant it may seem, making the Japanese in turn a pleasure to watch. Garbage collectors rush around with the purpose and exactitude of military sergeants, elevator operators of major department stores bow endlessly and yet cheerfully to streams of customers, restaurant workers shout enthusiastic greetings of welcome to everyone who walks in the door, and taxi drivers wear white gloves and use feather dusters to wipe unseen dirt from their shiny cabs. Even gas-station attendants act as though their job was the most important one on earth, ushering cars up to the pumps, filling tanks, washing windows and outside mirrors, emptying ashtrays, bowing and then stopping traffic so customers can ease back into the street, all in a matter of a few minutes.

But one of the most rewarding aspects of life in Tokyo is that the city, despite its size and apparent disorder, is actually very orderly. The Japanese thrive on routine and predictability, and once foreigners get used to the annoyances and restrictions that such an existence demands, the rest of the world begins to seem woefully out of step, uncivilized, and even downright dangerous. There are few freedoms greater than being in a city that is relatively free of crime and vandalism. The public telephones all work, the subways run like clockwork, graffiti is nonexistent, and when store clerks hand back change in lump sums, no one even bothers to check the amount because intentional shortchanging is simply unheard of. If you inadvertently leave a bag in a restaurant, taxi, or even a subway station, chances are you'll see it again, everything intact.

That is not to say you won't suffer moments of great frustration. The majority of streets wind without rhyme or reason—and most of them are unnamed; major subway and train stations are mazes so vast and confusing that at times you'll despair of ever finding your way out again (see "Essentials & Recommended Reading" for hints on navigating Tokyo). If you don't understand Japanese, you'll have no way of knowing whether that shop in front of you sells traditional Japanese sweets or pornographic comics. And Japanese who don't speak English may be reluctant to help you, simply out of embarrassment. Therefore, accept it that you will get lost; but take solace from the fact that even the Japanese get lost, and try to look at everything that happens as an adventure.

In Tokyo, it helps greatly if you have an undying sense of humor and a relish for the ridiculous and absurd.

HISTORY

For most of Japanese history, the action has taken place in the southern part of the country, in Kyushu and the plains and hills around Kyoto, which served as the nation's capital for more than a thousand years. And what a tumultuous history it's been—civil wars, assassinations, intrigues, and takeovers. Times were especially turbulent from about 1200 through the 1500s, when *daimyo* (feudal lords) throughout the land staked out fiefdoms and strove in vain for supremacy, leaving vicious civil wars and confusion in their wakes. Not unlike barons in medieval Europe, daimyo had absolute control over the people who lived in their fiefdoms and were aided in battles by an elite warrior caste, the *samurai*.

In the second half of the 16th century, several brilliant military strategists rose to power, but none proved as shrewd as Ieyasu Tokugawa, a statesman so skillful in eliminating his enemies that his heirs would continue to rule Japan for the next 250 years, bringing the nation an unprecedented time of peace. It was with him that Tokyo's history began.

For centuries, present-day Tokyo was nothing more than a rather obscure village called Edo, which means simply "mouth of the estuary" or "waterfront." Then, in 1590, Ieyasu acquired eight provinces surrounding Edo, much of it marsh and wilderness, with little fresh water available. Undaunted, Ieyasu chose Edo as his base and immediately set to work correcting the land's shortcomings by reclaiming land, building a conduit for fresh water, and constructing a castle surrounded by moats.

In 1603, Ieyasu succeeded in defeating all his rivals in a series of brilliant battles, becoming shogun, or military leader, over all of Japan. He declared the sleepy village of Edo the seat of his shogunate government, leaving the emperor intact but virtually powerless in Kyoto. He then set about expanding Edo Castle to make it the most impressive and largest castle in the land, surrounding it with an ingenious system of moats that radiated out from the castle in a great swirl, giving him access to the sea and thwarting enemy attack.

For even greater protection and to ensure that no daimyo in the distant provinces could grow strong enough to challenge him, the Tokugawa government ordered every daimyo to reside in Edo for a prescribed number of months every other year, thus keeping the feudal lords under the watchful eye of the shogunate.

Furthermore, all daimyo were required to leave their families in Edo as permanent residents, to serve as virtual hostages. By expending so much time and money traveling back and forth and maintaining residences in both the provinces and Edo, a daimyo would have found it very difficult to wage war. And as though that weren't enough, Ieyasu even dictated where daimyo lived in Edo. Those most loyal to Tokugawa were given land closest to the main gate, while those who had fought against him were given land farther out. There were as many as 270 daimyo in Japan in the 17th century, with each one owning several mansions in Edo for family members and retainers, complete with elaborate compounds and expansive landscaped gardens. Together with their samurai, who made up almost half of Edo's population in the 17th century, the daimyo and their entourage must have created quite a colorful sight on the dusty streets of old Edo.

After assuring its dominance on the home front, the Tokugawa government consolidated its power even more by closing its doors to the outside world. Fearing the spread of Western influence and Christianity in Japan and wishing to monopolize foreign trade, the Tokugawa shogunate adopted a policy of complete isolation in 1633, forbidding foreigners to enter Japan and the Japanese to leave. Those who defied the strict decrees paid with their lives. Incredibly, Japan's isolation from the rest of the world lasted more than 200 years.

The Edo Period (1603–1867) was a remarkable time in Japanese history. To cater to the needs of the shogun, daimyo and samurai, merchants and craftsmen from throughout Japan swarmed to Edo. To accommodate them, hills were leveled and marshes filled in, creating what is now the Ginza, Shimbashi, and Nihombashi. The population of Edo grew quickly, expanding from 562,000 inhabitants in 1731 to 1.3 million by 1787, making it one of the largest cities in the world (in comparison, in 1800 London had only 860,000 inhabitants; New York 60,000). Although it was a time of political stability, the price every individual paid for such security was drastic curtailment of personal freedom, with behavior, manner, and dress strictly dictated by the shogunate government. Society was divided into four distinct classes: the court nobles, the samurai, the farmers, and the merchants. Although the nobles occupied the most exalted social position, it was the samurai who wielded the real power, for they were the only ones allowed to carry weapons.

At the bottom of the social ladder were the merchants and townspeople. They were allotted land in Nihombashi and beyond, living even then in incredibly crowded conditions that make present-day Tokyo look absolutely spacious. Most townspeople lived in squalid tenements, which were typically long row houses constructed of wood and facing narrow meter-wide alleys, with open sewers running down the middle. Family homes were unimaginably small, consisting of a tiny entryway which also doubled as the kitchen and a single room about 100 square feet in size. Toilets and bathhouses were communal, and everyone pretty much knew everyone else's business.

Since most of the city was built of wood, it goes without saying that fires were a constant threat. In fact, rare indeed was the person who didn't lose his house at least several times during his lifetime. Between 1603 and 1868, Edo witnessed almost 100 major conflagrations, not to mention countless smaller fires. One of the biggest fires occurred in 1657, after a period of severe drought which had plagued the city for almost three months. Buffeted by strong winds, the flames ignited wooden homes and thatched roofs like tinder, raging for three days and reducing three-fourths of the city to smoldering ruins. More than 100,000 people lost their lives. When the smoke cleared, most of the castle, hundreds of daimyo mansions, shrines, and temples, and thousands of townspeople's homes were gone.

Despite such setbacks, the merchants of Tokyo grew in such number and became so wealthy that new forms of luxury and entertainment arose to accommodate them. Kabuki drama and woodblock prints became the rage, while stone and porcelain ware, silk brocade for elaborate and gorgeous kimono, and lacquerware were elevated to wondrous works of art. Japan's most famous pleasure district was an area to the northeast of Edo called Yoshiwara, the "floating world of pleasure," where rich merchants spent fortunes to cavort with beautiful courtesans.

By the mid-19th century it was clear that the feudal system was outdated. Although merchants were relegated the bottom rung of the social ladder, in truth they wielded so much economic power that money rather than rice became the primary means of exchange. Many samurai families, on the other hand, were on the brink of poverty. Discontent with the shogun grew widespread.

In 1854, Commodore Matthew C. Perry of the U.S. Navy succeeded in forcing the shogun to sign an agreement granting America trading rights, bringing Japan's two centuries of isolation to a close. Then, in 1868, the 15th Tokugawa shogun, Yoshinobu, stepped down from power and restored the Emperor Meiji as ruler. This historic event is called the Meiji Restoration, a landmark in Japanese history. The feudal era had come to an end.

Rather than remain in Kyoto, Emperor Meiji decided to claim Edo for his own, proclaiming it the imperial capital and renaming it Tokyo, or "Eastern Capital." The ensuing years, known as the Meiji Period, were nothing short of remarkable as Japan progressed rapidly from a feudal agricultural society of samurai and peasants to an industrial nation. The samurai were stripped of their power and were no longer allowed to carry swords; a prime minister and cabinet were appointed; a constitution was drafted; and a parliament, called the Diet, was elected. The railway, the postal system, and even specialists and advisers were imported from the West. Between 1881 and 1898, as many as 6,177 British, 2,764 American, 913 Germans, and 619 French were retained by the Japanese government to help transform Japan into a modern society.

As the nation's capital, Tokyo was especially caught up in the frenzy for modernization. West was best, and everything from fashion and food to architecture was eagerly imported from abroad, while things Japanese were forgotten or impatiently pushed aside. The Ginza arose as the nation's showcase for Western living, with brick buildings, gas streetlamps, and planted trees.

Tokyo's transformation into a Western metropolis was speeded even more by an unexpected tragedy in 1923, when a massive earthquake measuring 7.9 on the Richter scale shook the city just before noon, as children were on their way home from school and housewives were busy cooking the noontime meal. The fires that erupted from the quake, known as the Great Kanto Earthquake, destroyed up to 30 percent of the city's buildings and claimed more than 100,000 lives. Disaster struck again during World War II, when incendiary bombs laid more than half the city to waste and killed another 100,000 people.

Perhaps unsurprising in a city used to natural calamities, Tokyo was quick to cart off the wartime rubble and begin anew. Within a decade after the war, the city was completely rebuilt, with no trace of the widespread destruction only 10 years before. Through a series of policies that favored domestic industries and shielded Japan against foreign competition, the country experienced rapid economic growth, with Tokyo riding the crest of the economic wave. By the 1960s—only a century after Japan had opened its doors to the rest of the world and embraced modernization—the country was a major industrial power. In 1964, in recognition of Japan's increasing importance, the Summer Olympic Games were held in Tokyo, thrusting the city into the international spotlight.

Since then, Tokyo has remained one of the world's foremost cities in finance and technology. Although the economic bubble of the 1980s has burst, sending the nation reeling into a major recession, its economy now seems on the rebound and Tokyoites once again have a guarded optimism about their future. It's a city full of vitality, humming with energy, and on the cutting edge of everything from the arts to the sciences. In a nation of overachievers, it has more than its fair share of intelligentsia, academics, politicians, businesspeople, writers, and artists. As the trendsetter for Asia and the primary role model for developing Asian nations, Tokyo has already plunged headfirst into the 21st century. The city is so wired and electric that you can feel it in the air.

WALKING TOURS

This guidebook is geared toward independent travelers who like being on their own, like to walk, and are interested in immersing themselves in the life around them—in short, a guide book for those who may not even normally use guide books. Those who do rely on guide books religiously will find this one a good complement, since it not only leads one from A to B but also tells what to look for along the way. Because of the city's size, the language barrier, and its confounding winding streets, a walking guide to Tokyo is not only useful; it's darn near a necessity. This is the book I wish I had had when I first moved to Tokyo.

Assuming that most readers will not embark on every walking tour in this book, it's clear that some selections must be made in customizing individual itineraries. For those with only a couple days to spare, I recommend starting early the first morning with a walking tour of Tsukiji (Walking Tour 3) and its fish market, followed by a boat trip to Asakusa with its famous temple (Walking Tour 4) and old downtown atmosphere. On subsequent days I recommend tours of Ginza (Walking Tour 2), Ueno (Walking Tour 5), and Harajuku & Aoyama (Walking Tour 6). Not only do these five tours cover the city's most famous attractions, but they also show the city at its diverse best. Ginza, Harajuku, and Aoyama are the city's showcase for hi-tech and fashion, while Asakusa and Ueno offer glimpses into traditional Japan.

As for the other walking tours, they cover both well-trodden and off-the-beaten-path parts of the city, all unique in their own way. Readers interested in older, more traditional neighborhoods will want to include Yanaka (Walking Tour 9) in their amblings, one of my favorite spots in all of Tokyo and rarely included in sightseeing tours of the city. Walking Tour 8 covers Nihombashi and Ningyocho, well established since the early Edo days as the city's commercial and pleasure centers and yet surprisingly off the beaten tourist track. Walking Tour 11, which covers another Edo-era part of the city, introduces the peripatetic to a wide mix of attractions and districts, including the city's historical museum, its sumo town, its wholesale district for dolls, and the nation's largest electric and electronic district. For fashion, nothing beats Shibuya (Walking Tour 12), Harajuku & Aoyama (Walking Tour 6), and the Ginza (Walking Tour 2). For more museums and a tour of the imperial gardens, readers should refer to Walking Tour 1. Ikebukuro (Walking Tour 13) is for those who have already seen much of the city and are ready to expand their horizons to this commuter hub, while Shinjuku (Walking Tour 7) and Akasaka (Walking Tour 10) are for those interested in Tokyo's nightlife.

For the most part, you'll want to devote the better part of a day to each walk, especially if you're interested in stopping at all the museums or shops along the way. Alternatively, you may wish to personalize the walks to fit your own needs and interests, skipping some shops and attractions and whittling the tours down. With this in mind, I've listed subway and train stations not only at the beginning and end of each walk but also those you'll pass along the way.

And if by chance you do complete all thirteen walking tours in this book, you will have seen almost all the city's attractions—and explored more of Tokyo than most Tokyoites ever see.

Common Terms

bashi: bridge
chome: subdivision of a *ku*
dori: street *or* avenue
ji: temple
ku: ward
machi: town
mon: gate
za: theater

AROUND THE IMPERIAL PALACE

Start: Tourist Information Center (TIC), 1-6-6 Yurakucho. Station: Hibiya, then exit A2 or A4; or Yurakucho, then the Hibiya exit.

Finish: Yasukuni Shrine, Yasukuni-dori. Station: Kudanshita.

Time: 4–5 hours, including stops along the way.

Best Times: Tuesday, Wednesday, or Thursday, when everything is open.

Worst Times: Monday, when museums are closed; Friday, when the Imperial East Garden is also closed.

Tokyo does not have a clearly defined central district or downtown, but its spiritual heart is firmly rooted here, near the business districts of Hibiya, Yurakucho, and Marunouchi. This, after all, is where you'll find the Imperial Palace, home of Japan's 125th emperor, and was also the site of the largest castle Japan had ever seen, built by Shogun Ieyasu Tokugawa in the first half of the 1600s. This, therefore, was the center of old Edo, the place where Tokyo had its humble beginnings almost 400 years ago. Looking at the huge office buildings that surround the palace grounds today, it's hard to imagine that most of this area was once nothing more than a swampy marsh, with the waters of Tokyo Bay lapping at nearby shores. Vigorous land reclamation, begun in the time of Ieyasu himself, altered the shape of the land, creating the Ginza, Tsukiji, and points beyond.

This walk takes you past the Imperial Palace and through its adjacent oasis, the East Garden, to several nearby museums and a shrine. You could walk the entire length of the tour in about two hours if you didn't stop, but plan on spending at least half a day if you wish to take advantage of some of the worthwhile museums along the way.

• • • • • • • • • • • • • • • •

A good place to begin a tour of Tokyo is at the:

1. **Tourist Information Center,** where you should pick up a map of the city and stock up on pamphlets and brochures of Tokyo if you haven't already done so. It's open Monday through Friday from 9am to 5pm and on Saturday from 9am to noon.

Take a left out of the TIC. If you need to change money, look for the sign across the street for American Express. Just past it, on the side street that runs past American Express, is the American Pharmacy, which opened more than 40 years ago with the goal of introducing American products to Japan and is still a good place to shop for those hard-to-find toiletries, cosmetics, and distinctly American products, such as Colgate, greeting cards in English, stenographer notebooks, and even peanut butter and granola bars. It also carries *Tokyo Journal,* a monthly city magazine that describes what's going on in and around the city.

Otherwise, after taking a left from the TIC, take a left at the first side street. On your right you'll soon pass the:

2. **Takarazuka Theater,** home of a world-famous all-female troupe called the Takarazuka Kagekidan which stages elaborate revues with dancing, singing, and gorgeous costumes. The first Takarazuka troupe formed back in 1912

in a resort near Osaka and gained instant notoriety because it was all women, just as Kabuki is all men. Its audience is made up almost entirely of women, mainly middle-aged housewives. Performances are held six or seven months a year, generally March, April, July, August, November, and December, and sometimes June.

Straight ahead, at the T-intersection, is the Imperial Tower. If you take a left here, just before the overhead tracks on the left-hand side of the street is the:

3. **Sakai Kokodo Gallery,** 1-2-14 Yurakucho, which claims to be the oldest woodblock-print (ukiyo-e) shop in Japan. First opened in 1870 in Kanda by the present owner's great-grandfather, it is now tended by the fourth generation of the Sakai family and is a great place for original prints, as well as reproductions of such great masters as Hiroshige and Hokusai. Incidentally, the Sakai collection of woodblock prints is so vast, that the family has its own private woodblock-print museum in Matsumoto, located in the Japan Alps. The shop is open daily from 10am to 7pm.

Across the street from the gallery is the:

4. **Imperial Hotel,** one of Tokyo's best-known first-class hotels. Although the present hotel dates from 1970 with a 31-story tower added in 1983, the Imperial's history goes back to 1922, when it opened as a much smaller hotel designed by Frank Lloyd Wright. Made of brick, tile, and stone with intricate designs carved into its facade, it won lasting fame when it survived almost intact the 1923 earthquake that destroyed much of the rest of the city. It went on to become the preeminent hotel in Japan and was the hotel of choice for visiting foreign dignitaries and celebrities. Alas, what the earthquake was unable to destroy was no match for Tokyo's zeal for modernization, and that, coupled with the city's obsession with space, brought about the venerable building's demise in 1968, when it was torn down to make way for the present larger building. It's little consolation that part of the hotel's original facade is now on display in Meiji Mura, an architectural museum outside Nagoya. If you want, take solace in the hotel's lower-level shopping arcade, where you'll find expensive boutiques selling clothing, accessories, and pearls. If you make a reservation

The Tea Ceremony

Tea was introduced to Japan more than 1,000 years ago, brought from China where it was originally considered not a drink, but rather a powerful medicine used in fighting fatigue. Popular at first with Japanese Buddhist monks, who drank it to stay awake during long hours of meditation, it gradually became accepted among the upper classes of Japan. In the 16th century tea drinking was raised to an art with the practice of elaborate tea ceremonies, based on the principles of Zen and the spiritual discipline of the samurai. The tea ceremony was developed to free the mind of everyday stress through simplicity of movement and tranquil settings, thereby allowing one to achieve enlightenment and mental composure; it became so ritualized that one had to follow exact strictures in preparing, serving, and consuming the tea.

Today the tea ceremony, *cha-no-yu,* is still practiced in Japan as a form of disciplinary training for mental composure and as a kind of spiritual therapy, but is also used as a good way to learn about etiquette and manners. A traditional tea room is very tiny, with room for only five people, with an entrance so small that guests must crawl into the room. The bowl, caddy, and spoon used in the ceremony are passed around for inspection, and it would be considered most rude if the guests did not compliment the host on their beauty and design.

In Tokyo, your best bet for observing the tea ceremony is at one of the city's first-class hotels, with instruction in English. Although many foreigners may find the frothy green tea too bitter for their taste (sweets are served with the tea to offset its bitterness), watching the highly ritualized tea ceremony can be a fascinating experience. Since tea ceremonies offered by hotels are often booked by groups, be sure to call in advance to make a reservation.

in advance and pay a small fee, you can also join a tea ceremony, held in the hotel's Toko-an ceremonial chambers Monday to Friday from 10am to noon and again from

1 to 4pm. According to the hotel's brochure, "While an especially elaborate etiquette exists for both host and guest, it will suffice if our guests from overseas will simply sit as comfortably and as peacefully as possible on the tatami mat floors, noting the unique characteristics of the chambers, vestibules and pathways, preferably in silence. . . .Other objects normally noted are the actual vessels the tea is served in and the tools and accessories used in preparation."

Take a Break Since this area has a high concentration of office workers, who all eat lunch at the same time, avoid eating between noon and 1pm unless you want to wait in line. The Imperial Hotel's 13 restaurants and 4 bars offer everything from light snacks and French cuisine to Chinese food, sushi, and tempura. For a view of the surrounding area, however, head up to the 17th floor of the main building, where the **Rainbow Room** offers moderately priced all-you-can-eat lunch and dinner buffets with international cuisine daily from noon to 2:30pm and from 5:30 to 10pm. Next door at the sophisticated **Rainbow Lounge,** open daily from 11:30am to midnight, the view is even better, with panoramic views of Hibiya Park and the roofs of the Imperial Palace soaring above the greenery. Light snacks, including sandwiches, are served during lunch. Across the street in Hibiya Park, the **Matsumotoro** opened in 1903 and serves expensive French cuisine in its third-floor Bois de Boulogne, open daily from 11am to 9pm. On the ground floor is the casual Grill with outdoor seating, open daily from 11am to 8pm and offering inexpensive Western and Japanese food, most on display in its plastic-food case. Throughout Hibiya Park are also informal kiosks, small restaurants, and beer gardens, offering snacks and beverages, including one located in the northeast corner of the park with outdoor seating.

Across from the Imperial Hotel on Hibiya-Dori is:

5. **Hibiya Park,** which opened as the city's first Western-style park in 1903 and continues to serve as a popular urban oasis for office workers, shoppers, and families. Once the site of a feudal mansion, it contains dogwoods donated

Around the Imperial Palace

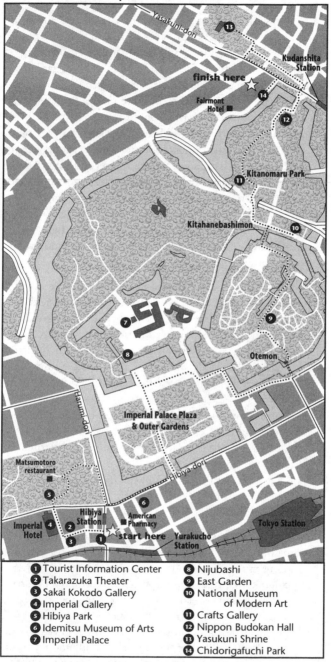

Yasakuni-dori

Kudanshita Station

finish here

Fairmont Hotel

Kitanomaru Park

Kitahanebashimon

Otemon

Imperial Palace Plaza & Outer Gardens

Harumi-dori

Matsumotoro restaurant

Hibiya-dori

Hibiya Station

American Pharmacy

Imperial Hotel

Yurakucho Station

start here

Tokyo Station

1. Tourist Information Center
2. Takarazuka Theater
3. Sakai Kokodo Gallery
4. Imperial Gallery
5. Hibiya Park
6. Idemitsu Museum of Arts
7. Imperial Palace
8. Nijubashi
9. East Garden
10. National Museum of Modern Art
11. Crafts Gallery
12. Nippon Budokan Hall
13. Yasukuni Shrine
14. Chidorigafuchi Park

by the United States in return for cherry trees given by the Japanese to Washington, D.C. In addition to a pond, children's playground, and beautifully laid-out flower garden, it also boasts several restaurants and beer gardens, a pleasant place to while away a sunny afternoon.

Exit from the northeast corner of Hibiya Park, crossing the Hibiya-dori and Harumi-dori intersection and heading north (the palace moat will be on your left). To your right you'll soon pass the Imperial Theater, which first opened in 1911 as Japan's first European-style theater and boasted such conveniences as advanced bookings, free programs, and modern restroom facilities. Today the theater stages such popular Western musicals as *Les Misérables* and *My Fair Lady* and other theatrical performances. If you turn right at the theater and walk midway down the block, you'll soon come to the entrance of the:

6. **Idemitsu Museum of Arts,** located on the third floor of the same building as the theater at 3-1-1 Marunouchi and offering beautiful views of the Imperial Palace grounds. Specializing in Japanese and Chinese pottery and ceramics, including old Imari and Kutani ware, it also displays Japanese calligraphy, ukiyo-e, screens and scrolls, and lacquerware. It's open every day except Monday from 10am to 5pm.

Continuing north on Hibiya-dori, turn left at the first stoplight and cross over the moat, where you'll find yourself in the Imperial Palace Plaza and Outer Garden, a spacious park noted for its open lawns and pine trees and popular with couples and people taking naps, oblivious to the traffic swirling around them. Straight ahead are the grounds of the:

7. **Imperial Palace,** home of Emperor Akihito, 125th emperor of Japan and descendant of the world's longest-reigning monarchy (incidentally, his marriage in 1959 to Michiko marked the first instance of a commoner marrying into the Imperial family). Built on the grounds where Edo Castle stood during the days of the Tokugawa shogunate, the original Imperial palace, made of wood, was completed in 1888 after the Imperial family moved from Kyoto to Tokyo but was destroyed, along with almost

everything else in the city, during air raids in 1945. The present palace was rebuilt in 1968 of ferroconcrete using principles of traditional Japanese architecture, and its grounds are open to the public only two days a year, on New Year's Day and on the emperor's birthday, December 23, when the Imperial family makes an appearance before the throngs. Even though they can't see much of the palace, Japanese tourists still make brief stops here daily to pay their respects. Console yourself with a camera shot of the palace grounds taken from the southeast side of:

8. **Nijubashi Bridge,** where you'll have a view of the double-arched stone bridge and the moat and turrets showing above the trees. The wide moat surrounds the palace and is lined with cherry trees, beautiful in spring and popular all year with jogging enthusiasts. It takes about an hour to circle the three miles around the palace if you were to walk at a leisurely pace. But by far the most worthwhile thing to do in the vicinity of the palace is to walk north around the moat to the Otemon Gate, once the main entrance to the shogun's castle. Today it serves as the main entrance to the:

9. **East Garden** (Higashi-Gyoen), one of Tokyo's best-kept secrets and occupying what was once the main grounds of Edo Castle. Amazingly enough in a city where everything is so expensive, admission to the garden is free and it's open every day except Mondays and Fridays from 9am to 4pm (you must enter by 3pm). Although the garden has been open to the public for more than two decades, many Japanese don't know it's here, and consequently it's hardly ever crowded, a great respite in the middle of the city.

As you walk through Otemon Gate, look for the mythical dolphins on the roof (thought to help ward off fires), the heavy gate, and the small walled entry courtyard, where any invaders could easily be overcome by occupant troops. As if that weren't enough, small slots built into the walls were designed for the slinging of arrows. Not far from the Otemon is the newly constructed Sannomaru Shozokan, which opened in 1993 with the purpose of displaying art treasures owned by the Imperial family, with changing exhibitions shown throughout the year. Behind the museum is Ninomaru, in my opinion the most beautiful part of the garden. Laid out in Japanese style with a pond, stepping stones, and winding paths, it is particularly beautiful when the wisteria, azaleas, irises, and other flowers are in bloom.

The highest spot of Higashi-Gyoen comprises the grounds of the Honmaru (the inner citadel), where Tokugawa's main castle once stood. Built in the first half of the 1600s, it was a massive complex, taking more than 30 years to complete and surrounded by a series of whirling moats and guarded by 23 watch towers and 99 gates. At its center was Japan's tallest building at the time, the five-story castle keep, soaring 168 feet above its foundations and offering an expansive view of Edo. This is where Ieyasu would have taken refuge, had his empire ever been seriously threatened. Although most of the castle was a glimmering white, the keep was black with a gold roof, which must have made quite a sight in old Edo as it towered above the rest of the city. Today all that remains of Tokugawa's castle are a few towers, gates, stone walls, moats, and the stone foundation of the keep. As you stand on top of the keep's foundation, imagine how different the view would have been back in the days of Edo—a marsh surrounded the Sumida River, and where Hibiya now stands was once a fishing village. Beyond it were the shores of the bay; what's Ginza today used to be completely under water.

☕ Take a Break   The **Honmaru Resthouse,** located in the Honmaru of the East Garden, is a good place to stop for a snack of ice cream or drinks. On its walls are photographs of the Imperial Palace's grounds and buildings taken decades ago, along with photographs of how the same buildings and grounds appear today, presenting a fascinating pictorial history.

Exit the East Garden via the Kitahanebashi mon Gate, located behind the castle keep's foundation. Cross over the busy street by using the pedestrian bridge and head downhill, where to your left you'll soon come to the:

10. **National Museum of Modern Art** (Tokyo Kokuritsu Kindai Bijutsukan), with its excellent collection of modern Japanese art, including Japanese-style paintings, Western-style paintings, prints, watercolors, drawings, and photographs, dating from the Meiji Period onward. A few

Western artists are also represented to provide a wider context, including works by Kokoschka, Jawlensky, Klee, and Richter. Japanese artists to watch for include Shiko Munahata, Seiki Kuroda, and Taikan Yokoyama. Exhibits are rotated from the permanent collection, so there's always something new to see. It's open Tuesday to Sunday from 10am to 5pm.

Take a right out of the museum and then another right over the bridge, which will take you to Kitanomaru Park (northern citadel), which used to be part of the Imperial Palace grounds and which opened to the public in 1969 to commemorate the 60th birthday of Emperor Showa. To your right you'll soon see the Science Museum, which isn't recommended since displays are in Japanese only. Rather, turn left and walk a minute or so until you get to the:

11. **Crafts Gallery** (Bijutsukan Kogeikan). Housed in a Gothic-style brick building constructed in 1910 as headquarters of the Imperial Guard, it collects the finest in contemporary crafts, including exquisitely made lacquerware, metalwork, ceramics, textiles, bamboo works, and glass by both Japanese and foreign artists, which it displays in rotating exhibitions. Highly recommended, it's open Tuesday to Sunday from 10am to 5pm.

From the museum turn left and head north, where you'll soon see the:

12. **Nippon Budokan Hall,** built for the 1964 Olympics as the arena for judo and other martial arts. The octagonal structure is based on the Horyuji Temple's Hall of Dreams in Nara, while its bronze-tiled roof is said to mimic the perfect symmetry of Mount Fuji and its foothills. Today a multipurpose hall used for sporting events and large concerts, it was first used for a concert in 1968—featuring the Beatles.

Circle clockwise around the Budokan until you come to a huge gate marking the edge of the park. Exit the park by walking over the moat and pedestrian bridge, where to your left you will soon see huge torii, reputedly the largest shrine gate in the world. It's the dramatic entrance to:

13. **Yasukuni Shrine,** built in 1869 under orders of Emperor Meiji and dedicated to Japanese war dead. During times of

war, soldiers were told that if they died fighting for their country their spirits would find glory here, and even today it's believed that the spirits of 2.5 million Japanese war dead are at home here, where they are worshipped as deities. During any day of the week, you're likely to encounter older Japanese here, paying their respects to friends and families who perished in World War II. Built in classic Shinto style, the shrine nevertheless becomes a center of controversy every August when World War II memorials are held here— in 1985, then prime minister Yasuhiro Nakasone caused a national uproar when he put in an appearance (some people thought it improper for a prime minister to visit a shrine so closely tied to Japan's nationalistic and militaristic past).

On the shrine's grounds is a small military museum, the Yushukan, containing weapons and memorabilia from the Sino-Japanese War, Russo-Japanese War, and both world wars. Included are samurai armor, swords, bows and arrows, tanks, guns, and artillery, as well as such disturbing displays as a human torpedo (a tiny submarine guided by one occupant and loaded with explosives) and a suicide-attack plane. But the most chilling displays are the endless photographs of war dead, some of them very young teenagers. In stark contrast to the somberness of the museum, temporary exhibits of beautiful ikebana (Japanese flower arrangements) and bonsai are also often held on the shrine's grounds, in glass display cases that ring the main hall.

Exit the shrine grounds by taking a left onto Yasukuni-dori and walking straight (east), where in approximately six minutes you'll come to:

14. **Chidorigafuchi Park** on your right, a half-mile-long promenade that runs along the west side of the palace moat and famous for its spectacular cherry trees in spring, which number almost 100. At its southern end is the National Cemetery for the Unknown Soldiers of World War II, where more than 330,000 urns for unidentified war dead have been interred. The promenade has benches along the way where you can stop and rest.

Otherwise, if you continue walking east on Yasukuni-dori, you will soon come to Kudanshita Station.

Take a Break   About halfway down Chidorigafuchi Park is the **Fairmont Hotel,** 2-1-17 Kudan-Minami, which has two moderately priced restaurants. Brasserie de la Verdure, open from 11am to 9:30pm daily, offers continental food, including seafood, pasta, and sandwiches, with a great view outside of the moat and cherry trees. If you wish, you can order just a drink. The French restaurant, Cerisiers, is slightly more formal and looks out onto a pleasant small garden with a waterfall. It's open for lunch daily from 11:30am to 2pm and for dinner from 6 to 9:30pm.

GINZA

Start: Tourist Information Center (TIC), 1-6-6 Yurakucho. Station: Hibiya, then exit A2 or A4; or Yurakucho, then the Hibiya exit.

Finish: World Magazine Gallery, 3-13-10 Ginza. Station: Higashi-Ginza.

Time: Allow one-and-a-half hours, not including stops along the way; otherwise, plan on spending about five hours for shopping, browsing, and eating.

Best Times: Monday through Friday, when most establishments are open. Also Sunday, when Chuo-dori becomes a pedestrian paradise, perfect for people-watching.

Worst Times: Thursday, when the Nihonshu Center selling sake is closed; Sunday, when some galleries and shops are closed; and the last few days of each month and the whole of August, when there are no Kabuki productions.

The Ginza is Tokyo's Fifth Avenue, its Champs-Elysees, the most famous, chic, and sophisticated shopping district in Japan. Appropriately enough, its name means "silver mint," a name which harks back to the days of Ieyasu Tokugawa, when the area was reclaimed from the sea and became home to a silver mint in 1612. After Japan opened its doors to the rest of the world in 1868, the Ginza emerged as the most Westernized district of Tokyo, with Western-style buildings displaying a curious assortment of imported goods, including Western clothing, beef, and other exotic items. There were brick buildings, gas streetlamps, wide paved avenues, brick sidewalks, and planted trees, a popular place for the upwardly mobile to shop and be seen.

Today the Ginza remains the hub of Japan's affluence and is the most fashionable shopping ground for Tokyo's well-to-do housewives. It boasts branches of all Japanese major department stores, as well as countless boutiques selling everything from designer clothes and accessories to kimono and traditional crafts. It also has more than 200 art galleries, giving it one of the highest concentration of art galleries in the world, and boasts a wide assortment of dining and entertainment establishments ranging from expensive restaurants and hostess clubs to yakitori bars, coffee shops, and cocktail lounges. The Ginza is worth a browse even if you can't afford to buy anything, especially on Sundays when Chuo-dori, the Ginza's main thoroughfare, is closed to traffic and becomes a pedestrian promenade with a festive-like atmosphere of sidewalk cafes, sidewalk bazaars, and families out for a weekend stroll. There's no longer a silver mint in the Ginza, but the coins keep rolling in.

• • • • • • • • • • • • • • • •

If you haven't already done so, stop by the:

1. **Tourist Information Center** to stock up on maps, pamphlets, and brochures of Tokyo. Take a right out of TIC, and then the first right, walking parallel to the overhead tracks. Note the small eating establishments tucked in under the arches of the tracks—they do a brisk and lively business with the many office workers of the district. About halfway down the block is an empty arch, home to makeshift yakitori stalls in the evening. You might want to return here after dark for an inexpensive meal and an atmosphere reminiscent of the 1950s, with the deep rumble of trains passing overhead.

At the first real street you come to (the Imperial Tower and Imperial Hotel will be to your right), turn left, where under the overhead tracks you'll see the:

2. **International Arcade,** a long arcade of tourist-oriented shops where you can look for such tax-free items as watches, pearls, kimono, yukata (cotton robes), T-shirts, woodblock prints, and souvenirs. If you're looking for old kimono, be sure to stop by Hayashi, which also carries new kimono, happi coats, yukata, obi (the sash used in securing kimono), and polyester versions. Although you can find lower prices elsewhere, this may be a good place to wander through if you're in a rush and don't have time to hunt around for things Japanese. Most shops are open daily from 10am to 6pm; some are closed on Sunday.

Cross to the other (east) side of the tracks and continue walking east in the direction of the Ginza (away from the elevated tracks), passing an elementary school and kindergarten. After a few short blocks you'll come to a big street with a traffic light, Sotobori-dori, where you should take a right and walk a couple of blocks, passing the first of many art galleries along the way. Note, too, the small curtains you may see hanging above the entryways of restaurants and shops. Called *noren*, they are often printed with the name of the establishment and are hung out front to let customers know the shop is open for business. When the shop closes for the day, the noren are always removed.

Soon, on your left, will be the:

3. **Takumi Craft Shop,** 8-4-2 Ginza (tel. 3571-2017), which often has a display of pottery outside its front door. This crafts shop stocks Japanese folk art, mainly pottery and textiles, as well as lacquerware, handmade paper objects, glassware, toys, noren, umbrellas, and some furniture. Hours are 11am to 7pm (to 5:30pm on national holidays); closed on Sunday.

Just past Takumi on the same side of the street is a strange sight that would be easy to overlook, the:

4. **Ginza Hachikan Jinja Shrine.** Founded about 300 years ago and dedicated to one of the gods of the sacred Outer Shrine of Ise, it's completely overshadowed by a building that was constructed—right over it! In land-hungry Japan, city lots are often too expensive for shrines alone. Unlike this shrine, however, most older shrines are moved to the

tops of office buildings. There are lots of rooftop shrines in the Ginza area.

Past the shrine, take a left at the next street and walk two short blocks to Namiki-dori, a narrow tree-lined lane where art galleries and exclusive boutiques alternate with pubs and hostess bars; return at night, and you'll find a completely different atmosphere. Among the galleries on Namiki-dori you might want to drop in on are:

5. **S. Watanabe,** 8-6-19 Ginza (tel. 3571-4684), dealing mostly in modern and antique woodblock prints and open Monday to Saturday from 9:30am to 8pm;

6. **Tokyo Gallery** (東京画廊), on the second floor of the Dai Go Shuwa Building at 8-6-18 Ginza (tel.3571-1808), a tiny gallery specializing in one-man shows of avant-garde art; and, farther down on the opposite side of Namiki Street,

7. **Gallery Ueda,** in the basement of the Asahi Building at 6-6-7 Ginza (tel. 3574-7553), which deals mainly with modern Japanese artists, many of whom incorporate traditional Japanese art in their works. It's open Monday to Saturday from 10:30am to 6:30pm.

At the end of Namiki-dori, on the right side, is:

8. **The Yoseido Gallery,** 5-5-15 Ginza (tel. 3571-1312), dealers in modern woodblock prints, etchings, silk-screens, copper plates, and lithographs. It's open Monday to Saturday from 10am to 6:30pm.

Take a Break For an inexpensive cup of coffee, a few shops down from S. Watanabe on Namiki-dori is one of the cheapest places in the Ginza, **Pronto,** 8-6-25 Ginza (tel. 3571-7864). A popular chain with branches throughout Tokyo, it's a coffee shop by day and a bar by night, open daily from 8am to 11pm. Nonsmokers, beware—smoke can be so heavy that you'll swear the place is burning down (according to a 1994 World Health Organization survey, 61% of Japan's adult males smoke). For a more sophisticated and unique atmosphere, head to the nearby **L'Ambre** (tel. 3571-9527), located on Sony Street a half block from the Sony Building, on a corner. Occupying

Ginza

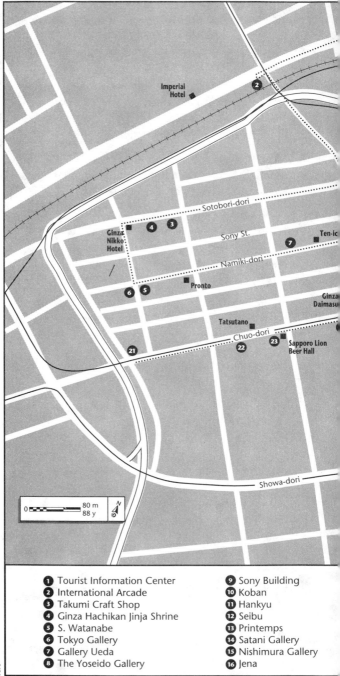

1 Tourist Information Center
2 International Arcade
3 Takumi Craft Shop
4 Ginza Hachikan Jinja Shrine
5 S. Watanabe
6 Tokyo Gallery
7 Gallery Ueda
8 The Yoseido Gallery
9 Sony Building
10 Koban
11 Hankyu
12 Seibu
13 Printemps
14 Satani Gallery
15 Nishimura Gallery
16 Jena

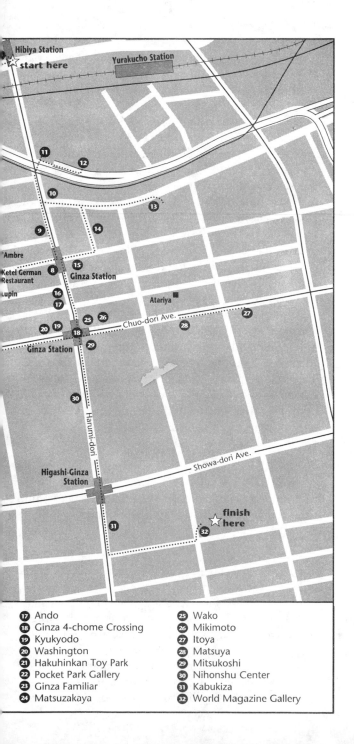

Hibiya Station
☆ start here

Yurakucho Station

⑪

⑫

⑩

⑬

⑨

⑭

°Ambre

Ketel German
Restaurant

⑧

⑮ **Ginza Station**

Lupin

⑯

⑰

Atariya ■

⑳ ⑲ ㉕ ㉖

⑱

Chuo-dori Ave. ㉘ ㉗

Ginza Station ㉙

㉚

Harumi-dori

**Higashi-Ginza
Station**

Showa-dori Ave.

☆ **finish
here**

㉛

㉜

⑰ Ando	㉕ Wako
⑱ Ginza 4-chome Crossing	㉖ Mikimoto
⑲ Kyukyodo	㉗ Itoya
⑳ Washington	㉘ Matsuya
㉑ Hakuhinkan Toy Park	㉙ Mitsukoshi
㉒ Pocket Park Gallery	㉚ Nihonshu Center
㉓ Ginza Familiar	㉛ Kabukiza
㉔ Matsuzakaya	㉜ World Magazine Gallery

a Gothic-looking building totally out of character for the Ginza, it's an old-fashioned coffee shop specializing in classical music, with seats so comfortable that you'll find a surprising number of office workers sacked out and slumbering away (hiding from their bosses, perhaps?). It's open Monday to Saturday from 11:30am to 11pm.

For something more substantial, **Ten-ichi (天一)**, located on Namiki-dori at 6-6-5 Ginza (tel. 3571-1949) is the main shop of a restaurant chain that first served tempura in Tokyo more than 50 years ago and still has one of the best reputations for delicately fried foods. It's open daily from 11:30am to 10pm. Also on Namiki-dori is **Ketel German Restaurant,** 5-5-14 Ginza (tel. 3571-4642), which has been offering an English menu of German food since 1930 and is open daily from 11:30am to 9:45pm. There are several possibilities for dining in the Sony Building, located on the corner of Harumi and Sotobori avenues, including the very expensive **Maxim's** (tel. 3572-3621), an art-nouveau carbon copy of the Parisian restaurant, open Monday to Saturday from 11:30am to 11pm; **Sabatini Di Firenze** (tel. 3573-0013), a formal and civilized Italian restaurant on the seventh floor with views of the Ginza and open daily from noon to 11pm; and the very casual and inexpensively priced **Al Dente** (tel. 3574-7470), which offers more than 30 different kinds of spaghetti daily from 11am to 9pm.

Namiki-dori empties onto Harumi-dori, a busy street that runs from Hibiya through the heart of the Ginza. Turn left here and go one short block to the:

9. **Sony Building,** 5-3-1 Ginza (tel. 3573-2371). This place is always crowded, primarily because its ground floor serves as a popular meeting place in the Ginza, especially in the early evening when couples or friends meet for dinner or drinks (nearly every district or neighborhood has a famous meeting spot that everyone knows, since Tokyoites usually socialize outside the home and therefore meet friends at public places). As you might expect, Sony displays its products in showrooms on almost every floor. Stop here to see all the latest in everything from the Discman and camcorders to car navigation systems. It's open daily from 11am to 7pm.

Catty-corner from the Sony Building, on the other side of Harumi-dori, is a brick:

10. **Koban,** one of the most famous police boxes in Japan. The Koban system originated during the Edo Period, to protect townpeople from overzealous samurai who, no longer having any battles to wage, were keen on practicing their fighting techniques and testing the effectiveness of new swords by attacking unwitting passersby (during the Edo Period, only samurai were allowed to carry swords and were legally allowed to kill any commoner who behaved disrespectfully). There are now koban all over Japan, but this one, with its copper-plated peaked roof and red-and-brown striped walls is larger than most and certainly one of the most stylish. Stop here if you need directions.

Behind the Koban are two department stores:

11. **Hankyu** (tel. 3575-2233), on the left, open every day except Thursday from 10am to 7pm, and

12. **Seibu** (tel. 3286-0111), with one building selling clothing and accessories (including designs of Giorgio Armani, Yohji Yamamoto, Comme des Garcons, Kenzo, Issey Miyake, Sonia Rykiel, Jasper Conran, Katharine Hamnett, and Donna Karan) and the other specializing in interior design and kitchenware. It's open weekdays from 11am to 8pm and weekends from 11am to 7pm, closed the second and third Tuesdays of every month.

Altogether there are seven large department stores in the Ginza, each closed on different days of the week so you can always find several that are open. Sundays are the busiest days; the busiest months tend to be July and December, when the Japanese exchange mid-year and year-end gifts. Originally a religious custom, the practice today involves mainly business people, who send gifts to superiors and customers as an expression of thanks to those who have afforded assistance. Food and beverages are the most popular gifts. If you're looking for bargains, head for a department store's sales or exhibition floor, usually on an upper floor and offering monthly sales ranging from designer clothes and handbags to golfing accessories, shoes, and lingerie.

Down the street from these two department stores is a relative newcomer on the Ginza scene:

13. **Printemps,** 3-2-1 Ginza (tel. 3567-0077), a branch of Paris's fashionable Au Printemps but with a selection more suited to the Japanese. A fun store popular with Tokyo's young generation, it sells the fashions of Hiroko Koshino (one of Japan's up-and-coming young designers), Takeo Kikuchi, Jurgen Lehl, Kenzo, and other well-known design houses. An annex sells goods for the home. It's open from 10am to 7pm; closed Wednesday.

Heading back towards Harumi-dori, on the corner of a small side street, is:

14. **Satani Gallery,** located in the first basement of the Daini Asahi Building at 4-2-6 Ginza (tel. 3564-6733). It presents paintings and sculptures of young Japanese contemporary artists, and also represents such well-known international artists as Christo, Max Ernst, Paul Klee, and Joan Miro. It's open Monday to Saturday from 11am to 6pm.

Just around the corner, on Namiki-dori, is another gallery, the:

15. **Nishimura Gallery,** located in a basement at 4-3-13 Ginza (tel. 3567-3906), which features an even mixture of Japanese and foreign (mainly British) painters and sculptors, including David Hockney and Funakoshi Katsura.

Return to Harumi–dori, turning left and heading away from the elevated tracks. On your right is:

16. **Jena,** 5-6-1 Ginza (tel. 3571-2980), a bookstore that carries foreign titles on its third floor, including magazines, novels, and special-interest publications. It's smaller than Maruzen in Nihombashi or Kinokuniya in Shinjuku, but you might want to stop for a quick look, especially if you're interested in books on Japan. It's open Monday to Saturday from 11am to 7:30pm and Sunday from noon to 7pm.

Next door is:

17. **Ando,** 5-6-2 Ginza (tel. 3572-2261), which opened in 1880 and offers what is probably the largest selection of cloisonne in town, including jewelry, vases, and plates. It's open Monday through Friday from 9am to 6pm and Saturday and Sunday from 11am to 7pm.

Continue on Harumi-dori until you come to Chuo-dori. This intersection, called the:

18. **Ginza 4-chome Crossing** (or sometimes just Ginza Crossing), is the heart of the Ginza, with department stores Wako and Mitsukoshi, fashion building Sanai, and the Nissan Ginza Gallery on its corners. The subway station here is serviced by three subway lines—the Hibiya, Ginza, and Marunouchi lines. Take a right here, passing the circular, glass building, Sanai, with boutiques on several floors, and:

19. **Kyukyodo,** 5-7-4 (tel. 3571-4429), a well-known and established stationery shop popular with Japanese housewives. First established in Kyoto in 1663 as a chemist's shop, the Tokyo store has been here for more than a century, selling Japanese paper, incense, calligraphy brushes, ink, fans, and fountain pens. It's open Monday to Saturday from 10am to 8pm and Sunday and holidays from 11am to 7pm. Farther down the street, also on the right, is the five-story:

20. **Washington,** 5-7-7 Ginza (tel. 3572-5911), one of the largest shoe stores in Tokyo, with large and small sizes available on the fifth floor. Hours here are 10:30am to 8pm daily.

If you continue walking on Chuo-dori all the way to the end where the overhead expressway is, you'll come to:

21. **Hakuhinkan Toy Park,** 8-8-11 Ginza (tel. 3571-8008), one of Japan's largest toy stores with a wide range of games, stuffed animals, toys, and other diversions, including video games you can play. It's open daily from 11am to 8pm.

Cross the street and walk back on the other side of Chuo-dori toward the Ginza Crossing. In the next block on your right is:

22. **Pocket Park Gallery,** 7-9-15 Ginza (tel. 3573-1401), sponsored by Tokyo Gas. Offering a nice change of pace from the usual Ginza shops, this small place features a ground-floor coffee shop, as well as two exhibit spaces dedicated to changing displays of architectural and industrial design. To the layman it may sound boring, but past shows have included unusual inventions, including bicycles that can also ride across water (called, amusingly, "Waterfowl"),

a dual wheelchair/bike that allows an abled person to pedal while the disabled sits in front in a wheelchair, and a step ladder that allows the user to inch forward by winding a handle, without having to step off the ladder. On the third floor is an architectural library, with many books in English. Entrance to the gallery is free, so it's worth a quick spin through to see what's on display. It's open every day except Wednesday from 10:30am to 7pm.

Feeling pooped? Next to the Pocket Park Gallery is a statue of Ryoichi Sasakawa, chairman of the Japan Ship-building Industry Foundation, depicted here climbing the 785 steps of Kompira Shrine in Shikoku—carrying his 82-year-old mother on his back. That must have won him a lot of points with the shrine gods. After passing the Sapporo Lion Beer Hall, in the next block on the right is:

23. **Ginza Familiar,** 6-10-16 Ginza (tel. 3574-7111), an expensive clothing store for babies and kids who have everything (including rich parents). You could spend a small fortune dressing fashion fledglings here; on the top floor are toys, including toys from around the world, at inflated prices. It's open daily from 11am to 7pm.

Just past Ginza Familiar is another department store:

24. **Matsuzakaya,** 6-10-1 Ginza (tel. 3572-1111), popular with middle-aged housewives and open from 10am to 7pm, closed most Wednesdays.

Take a Break Next to Washington shoe store on Chuo-dori is **Tatsutano (立田野),** 7-8-7 Ginza (tel. 3571-1840), a Japanese sweet shop popular with house-wives for its vanilla and sweet-bean-paste ice cream, cold and sweet somen (noodles), and fruit concoctions. Choose what you want from the plastic-food display out front. It's open daily from 11:30am to 7:30pm. If beer is more to your taste, you can't go wrong at the **Sapporo Lion Beer Hall** on Chuo-dori, 7-9-20 Ginza (tel. 3571-2590), which opened as one the country's first beer halls in 1934. It features a mock Gothic interior, an English menu, and Sapporo beer. For moderately priced Japanese food, head for **Ginza Daimasu (銀座大増),** a 60-year-old restaurant located on Chuo-dori across from the Matsuzakaya department store at 6-9-6 Ginza (tel. 3571-3584). Its set meals, especially lunches, are a good buy; choose from the plastic-food display case out front.

Back at Ginza Crossing, cross the intersection walking towards the older building with the clock on top, a Ginza landmark. That's the:

25. **Wako department store,** one of the few buildings in the Ginza to survive World War II bombing raids. Erected in 1932 and famous for its clock tower, graceful curved facade and innovative shop windows, it's owned by the Hattori family, founders of the Seiko watch company. Its ground floor carries a wide selection of Seiko watches and clocks, while the upper floors carry imported and domestic fashions and luxury items, with prices to match. One of the classiest stores around, it's open Monday to Friday from 10am to 5:30pm and Saturday from 10am to 6pm.

A few shops down from Wako, on Chuo-dori, is:

26. **Mikimoto,** 4-5-5 Ginza (tel. 3535-4611), one of the most famous names in cultured pearls. Its founder was Koichi Mikimoto, who after more than 10 years of frustrating experimentation and research became the first to produce a really good cultured pearl back in 1905. He once said to Emperor Meiji, "I want to adorn the neck of every woman in the world with a pearl necklace." The pearls sold by this main shop, open every day except Wednesday from 10:30am to 6pm, are expensive but of top quality.

Farther down Chuo-dori on the other side of the street is:

27. **Itoya,** 2-7-15 Ginza (tel. 3561-8311), established in 1904 as a stationery store and still one of Tokyo's best-known office-supply shops. Open Monday to Saturday from 9:30am to 7pm and stocked with stationery, Japanese paper, pens, staplers, and nifty desk-top gadgets, it also prints business cards in about a week. You're a nonentity in Japan without business cards (called *meishi*) so if you've arrived without any or wish to have new ones printed with Japanese on the reverse side (an unusual souvenir of Japan), you might consider leaving an order here. Keep in mind that when exchanging meishi, you should present it with both hands, so that it's right side up and immediately readable to

the person you're giving it to. A meishi is presented first by the lower person on the totem pole, and it's proper etiquette to study the meishi for a few seconds—putting it right away without glancing at it would be considered most rude.

28. **Matsuya,** 3-6-1 Ginza (tel. 3567-1211), the Ginza branch of a famous Japanese department store and one of my favorites. It has a good selection of Japanese folkcraft items and souvenirs, kitchenware, and beautifully designed contemporary household goods. I always make a point of dropping by the seventh floor's Design Collection, which displays items from around the world selected by the Japan Design Committee as examples of fine design. Included have been the Alessi teapot from Italy, Braun razors and clocks, and Porsche sunglasses. If I were buying a wedding gift, Matsuya is one of the first places I'd look. It's open from 10am to 7pm, closed Tuesdays.

Located right on Ginza 4-chome Crossing is:

29. **Mitsukoshi,** 4-6-16 Ginza (tel. 3562-1111), the Ginza branch of the famous Mitsukoshi in Nihombashi and popular with young shoppers. It's open from 10am to 7pm, closed most Mondays.

Cross Harumi-dori and turn left in front of the Nissan Ginza Gallery. Just a stone's throw from the intersection, to the right, is the:

30. **Nihonshu Center (日本酒センター),** 5-9-1 Ginza (tel. 3575-0656), which sells something dear to my heart—the Japanese rice wine, sake (look for the store's sign that says Sakespo 101). With information on the thousands of different kinds of sake made in Japan, it carries a different selection every month. For a nominal fee, visitors can sample five different brands of sake and then keep their cup as a souvenir. What a deal! It's open every day except Thursdays and holidays from 10:30am to 6pm.

Continue walking along Harumi-dori, away from the Ginza Crossing, crossing the next big street, Showa-dori, where to your left you will see the unmistakable:

31. **Kabukiza,** 4-12-14 Ginza (tel. 3541-3131, or 5565-6000 for reservations), Tokyo's most famous Kabuki theater. With an impressive Momoyama-style facade influenced by

16th-century castle architecture, the present structure is a remake of the 1924 original building. Seating almost 2,000, it features the usual Kabuki stage fittings, including a platform that can be raised and lowered below the stage for dramatic appearances and disappearances of actors, a revolving stage, and a runway stage extending into the audience.

Kabuki's name stems from the word "Kabuku," meaning a deviation from normal behavior, a reference to its beginnings in the early 16th century when a troupe of women in Kyoto found a ready audience for their simple erotic dances. Since some of the dancers were prostitutes, and some of the dances were quite lewd, the shogun soon decided that the dances were too vulgar and he banned all women from performing. Young boys took over the roles of women, but it wasn't long before they too were banned from the stage, since their presence was regarded by the shogun as an unwelcome encouragement of sodomy, widely practiced by members of both the warrior class and the clergy. That left only men to play the roles of both male and female, which they do to this day.

Kabuki has changed little in the past 100 years. Altogether, there are more than 300 Kabuki plays, most written before this century, with universal themes centering on love, revenge, and the conflict between duty and personal feelings. Costumes are usually gorgeous and the stage settings often fantastic, but one of the more arresting things about a Kabuki performance is the audience itself. Kabuki has always been for the masses, and the audience can get quite lively, with yells, guffaws, and laughter from spectators. In fact, old woodcuts of cross-eyed men apparently stemmed from Kabuki—when things got too rowdy, actors would stamp their feet and strike a cross-eyed pose in an attempt to get the audience's attention.

Of course, you won't be able to understand what's being said. Indeed, because much of Kabuki drama dates from the 18th century, even the Japanese sometimes have difficulty understanding the language. But that doesn't matter—it's great entertainment. The Kabukiza stages about eight or nine productions a year, with each production beginning its run between the first and third of each month and running about 25 days daily from 11 or 11:30am to about 9pm; note that there are no shows in August. If you don't have much time, I suggest you head to the fourth floor, where at a discounted price you can watch part of a program (entrance to the fourth floor is to the left of the main entrance). Seats here are available on a first-come, first-served basis for the one- to two-hour shows, and English programs are available. You can, of course, also purchase regular tickets, for which there's the extra advantage of English-language earphones available for rent that provide a running commentary on the story, the music, actors, stage properties, and other aspects of Kabuki. In any case, I strongly suggest that you either buy a program or rent earphones; it will add to your enjoyment of the play immensely.

If no production is being staged or you have an hour or so to kill before the next program, I suggest you walk past the Kabukiza, turn left, and walk to the second street. Here, on the corner, is the hard-to-miss:

32. **World Magazine Gallery,** 3-13-10 Ginza (tel. 3545-7227), a striking pink-and-white striped building that serves as headquarters of a Tokyo publishing house. On the second floor is a reading gallery, where more than 1,200 magazines from 40 countries around the globe are on display. Magazines are for reading here only, either at one of the many tables available or at the coffee shop. This is a great place to catch up on the news from back home or to see the latest edition of your favorite magazine, whether it's a sports, fashion, art, hobby, or interior design publication. The Magazine Gallery is open Monday through Saturday from 11am to 7pm.

From here the closest station is Higashi-Ginza, located in front of Kabukiza theater.

Take a Break After a tiring day of window shopping in the Ginza, I like to reward myself with a drink or light snack at **Hill Colonial Garden,** a coffee-and-dessert shop on the second floor of Mitsukoshi department store with windows overlooking the bustling Ginza Crossing intersection. It's open daily from 9:30am to 11:30pm. If you prefer something quieter and more subdued, a great bar in the Ginza is **Lupin (ルパン),** 5-5-11 Ginza (tel. 3571-0750), located in an alley behind the German restaurant Ketel. Opened in 1928 as one of the first basement bars, it has changed little over the decades and is so quiet you can hear yourself think—as though the world of jukeboxes and stereos has passed it by, no music is ever played here. A very civilized place, it's open Monday to Saturday from 5 to 11pm.

For a livelier evening, what better way to end a day than at a yakitori-ya, a drinking establishment that sells skewers of chicken and other snacks, along with the requisite beer. **Atariya (当りや),** 3-5-17 Ginza (tel. 3564-0045), is a fun, convivial place with a friendly staff and an English menu and is located on the small side street that runs behind the Wako department store (look for the red lantern outside Atariya's door). It's open Monday through Saturday from 4:30 to 10:30pm. For more substantial dining, try Shabusen, located on Chuo-dori between Ginza Crossing and Matsuzakaya department store, on the second floor of the Core Building at 5-8-20 Ginza (tel. 3571-1717). Serving shabu-shabu and sukiyaki, it's open daily from 11am to 9:30pm. For more dining suggestions, refer to the "Take a Break" mentioned earlier in this walk.

TSUKIJI

Start: Tsukiji Honganji Temple, Shin Ohashi-dori. Station: Tsukiji, then the Tsukiji Honganji Temple exit.

Finish: Hama Rikyu Garden. Station: Shimbashi.

Time: Plan on spending about three to four hours, not including Take a Break.

Best Times: 5am to 10am Tuesday through Saturday, when the fish market is in full swing and Hama Rikyu Garden is open.

Worst Times: Monday, when Hama Rikyu Garden is closed, and Sunday or any afternoon, when the fish market is closed. In any case, avoid traveling on the subway during rush hour, which is generally from 7:30 to 9am on weekdays. If these are the times that best fit your schedule, take a taxi to Tsukiji.

If you've already flown halfway around the world to Tokyo, you already know what it's like to awaken bright-eyed and ready for action in the darkness of pre-dawn, your body still attuned to the time zone you left behind. Wide awake by 4 or 5am, you probably stayed in bed, tossing and turning and counting the minutes until the hotel coffee shop opened at 6am. Then came another few agonizingly slow hours, as you waited for your 10am business meeting or for the capital's shops and museums to open their doors. What a waste.

Instead, you should have risen in the darkness, dressed in comfortable clothing and a pair of casual walking shoes (rubber boots are best, but who packs those?), and headed straight for Tsukiji. There, in a cavernous hangar-like covered building, is one of Tokyo's most impressive sights, the Tsukiji Fish Market. It's a must-see, and since you must see it in the wee hours of the morning to witness it at its best, what better time to head there than your first sleepless morning in the capital?

Properly speaking, Tsukiji refers to an entire district, sandwiched in between the swank Ginza area and Tokyo Bay with its wharves and port. Its origins stretch back to the 1657 fire which destroyed much of Tokyo, when the Tokugawa shogunate decided that the best way to prevent the outbreak of more devastating fires was to provide more space between buildings and thereby eliminate the cramped wooden quarters that had so readily fueled the flames. Part of this plan was reclamation of land from Tokyo Bay, from which Tsukiji was born. Tsukiji, in fact, means "reclaimed land." How appropriate that this area, once covered with water, is now home to the largest fish market in the nation.

Just two subway stops from the Ginza, Tsukiji Market takes place Monday to Saturday from approximately 3am to around noon but is best visited between 4 and 8am. However, keep in mind that if you set out too early, you may find yourself at the area's other major attraction, Hama Rikyu Garden, ahead of its 9am opening. I suggest, therefore, that you arrive in Tsukiji between 6 and 7am, well ahead of the subway rush-hour madness and in time to witness the market at its busiest. If getting up so early is a physical abomination, you should at least try to start this tour by 10am. There aren't a lot of attractions and sights along the way, but you'll want to spend at least an hour each at both the fish market and the garden.

Because Tsukiji is best seen in the morning and takes in less than a dozen sights, I suggest you couple it with an onward tour of Asakusa, covered in Walk 4. The reason is that ferries depart Hama Rikyu Garden approximately every hour for Asakusa, making it a logical next destination after Tsukiji. Not only does the 35-minute boat trip give you the chance to relax, but it also affords a unique view of Tokyo via the Sumida River.

• • • • • • • • • • • • • • • •

Our tour of Tsukiji begins at the:

1. **Tsukiji Honganji Temple,** a large ferroconcrete building on Shin Ohashi-dori. A branch of Kyoto's Nishi Honganji temple, this temple was built in 1934 by architect Chuta Itoh, also a noted archaeologist credited with discovering an ancient mountainside temple in China. In designing Tsukiji Honganji, which reflects distinct Hindu architecture and is the only East Indian–style Buddhist temple in Japan, Itoh hoped to increase Japanese appreciation of ancient Eastern cultures.

   You can see the temple's exotic interior by walking up the central steps to the main hall, open daily from 6am to 4pm. Most of the time you'll even find an English-speaking guide waiting for you, eager to give a short free lecture of the temple and its treasures. Most noteworthy is the Amida Buddha in the center altar. To the right is an image of Prince Shotoku, an enlightened leader who introduced Buddhism to Japan at the beginning of the 7th century.

   Upon exiting the temple, watch how people passing by are likely to pause in front of temple and give a slight bow as a sign of respect. Take a left out of the temple and walk straight to busy Harumi-dori, which runs through Tsukiji and the Ginza all the way to Hibiya. Turn right here, and after one short block you will come to:

2. **Kimuraya Shikki Ten,** 2-15-17 Tsukiji (tel. 3541-0151), on the right-hand side and the first of many kitchenware shops in the Tsukiji area. Because so many restaurateurs shop in Tsukiji for the freshest in fish and produce, the area abounds in wholesale and retail outlets selling pottery, lacquerware, kitchenware, and tableware. This shop, open Monday to Saturday from 7:30am to 5pm, specializes in lacquerware, with a large selection of traditional red and black trays, bowls, and chopsticks. Next door is:

3. **Iwama Chinaware,** 2-15-17 Tsukiji (tel. 3541-0070), a wholesale tableware shop where individual shoppers are welcome. It's open Monday to Saturday from 8am to 5pm. If these shops aren't yet open, you might want to return to them later in the morning.

Tsukiji

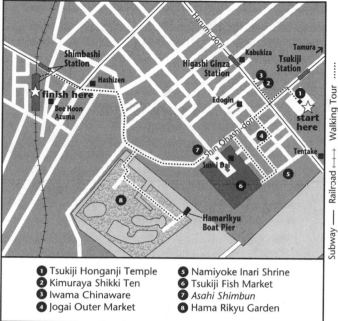

1 Tsukiji Honganji Temple
2 Kimuraya Shikki Ten
3 Iwama Chinaware
4 Jogai Outer Market
5 Namiyoke Inari Shrine
6 Tsukiji Fish Market
7 *Asahi Shimbun*
8 Hama Rikyu Garden

Subway ⎯ Railroad ⫫ Walking Tour ⋯⋯

Retrace your steps back to the Shin Ohashi–Harumi intersection and head for the covered sidewalk diagonally across the intersection. This is the beginning of the:

4. **Jogai Outer Market,** which serves the needs of the general public. Threaded through with tiny alleyways and open-fronted shops, it bustles with shoppers, bicycles, and men pushing carts, all part of an ageless scene that includes dazzling displays of fish, octopus, seaweed, fresh and pickled vegetables, knives, tofu, dried seafood, and much, much more. I suggest you walk aimlessly through the market, which is open Monday through Saturday from 4am to noon. In any case, try to end up at the opposite far corner of the outer market (or, from the Shin Ohashi–Harumi-dori intersection, walk south on Shin Ohashi-dori with the outer market on your left-hand side, turning left at the first crosswalk and stoplight and walking straight). Here, at the end of a T-intersection, is:

5. **Namiyoke Inari Shrine,** a tiny place of worship just outside the fish market. It was founded more than 300 years

ago, when much of Tsukiji was nothing more than mud flats, and is now Tsukiji's principal shrine. Chances are you'll see a local or two stop by to pay respects, perhaps to thank the powers that be for a particularly good deal at the fish market or to request the safe return of a fisherman. To the right of the main hall is a huge image of a dragon/dog's head, paraded through the neighborhood during the shrine's annual festival.

Take a left out of the shrine, walking over the bridge that marks the entrance to:

6. **Tsukiji Fish Market** (Uogashi). Steering clear of the crazy traffic of carts, forklifts, and wagons that zip every which way, head for the cavernous building to the left. This is the center of Japan's largest fish market, not surprising when you consider that 12 million people live in Tokyo and that the average Japanese eats 80 pounds of seafood a year. In fact, considering how important seafood is to the Japanese diet, I wouldn't be surprised to learn that this is the largest market for seafood in the world. Fish provides more than half the protein in a Japanese diet, and more than a thousand different varieties are consumed.

The action at Tsukiji Fish Market starts early, as trucks and boats arrive from about midnight to 3am, laden with fish caught around the world—from the waters off India, Brazil, Indonesia, China, Thailand, Malaysia, Mexico, and North America. Tuna, the Japanese favorite, is king of the market, with as many as 191 tons of fish auctioned off in a single day in Tsukiji. Bluefins, flown in fresh from the cold waters off Long Island or Canada, are the most valued and can weigh as much as 1,800 pounds. Less valuable tuna is shipped frozen. If you get here before the tuna auctions start at 5:30am, you'll find the huge bodies of tuna, each marked with a red number, laid out in the far left corner of the building, with wholesalers walking up and down between the rows, inspecting the tuna with flashlights, shaving off a bit of meat to test its texture, color, and smell, and jotting down the numbers of the best-looking specimens. The tails of each tuna have been cut off, so that experienced wholesalers can tell at a glance the fat content of the meat. The entire scene is bathed in a white, surrealistic mist that rises from the frozen carcasses.

Once the bidding of the auctions is complete, wholesalers transfer their purchases to their own stalls in the huge market; they subsequently sell their purchases to their regular customers, usually retail stores and restaurants. Altogether there are more than 1,200 vendors in Tsukiji market, each specializing in certain kinds of seafood, and they seem to stretch on forever. They sell salmon, crabs, lobster, shrimp, mackerel, tuna, sardine, squid, octopus, sea urchin, oysters, abalone, blowfish, eel, frog, and countless other creatures I can't identify.

From about 7 to 10am there's a lot going on—men in black rubber boots rushing wheelbarrows and carts through the aisles, hawkers shouting, knives chopping and slicing (some of the scenes are not for the fainthearted), housewives, professional chefs, and shopowners dodging each other on the wet stone floors. As a visitor you're welcome, but keep clear of the workers as they rush through their jobs. This is a good place to bring your camera—workers here seem to burst with pride when you single them out for a photograph.

Take a Break After having walked around for a while, you're probably ready for breakfast or lunch. As you might imagine, this market offers some of the freshest seafood anywhere, making it a great place for a meal of sashimi. Beside the covered market are rows of barrack-like buildings divided into sushi restaurants and shops related to the fish trade. To reach them, return to the bridge you crossed upon entering the market. Don't cross it, but rather turn left just in front of it, walking past some shops selling knives and other fish-related cooking products. To your left you will soon see numbered concrete barracks. There are dozens of tiny restaurants here, most nothing more than a single counter with a dozen stools. My favorite is **Sushi Dai,** or **寿司大** in Japanese (tel. 3542-1111), located in Building 6 on the third alley (which is the alley *after* the post office). It's the third shop on the right. Typical of the other sushi bars here, it consists of one counter, usually filled with people who work in the vicinity. Probably the easiest thing to do is to order the *seto,* a set sushi course. It's open Monday to Saturday from 5am to 2pm. If you want something a bit more refined, try **Edogin (江戸銀),** 4-5-1 Tsukiji (tel. 3543-4401), a well-known sushi restaurant offering lunch specials (called *teishoku*). It's located to the southwest of the Harumi and Shin Ohashi intersection, on a small side street, and is open Monday to Saturday from 11am to 9:30pm. If you've heard about the Japanese love affair with blowfish (*fugu*) and wish to take your chances with this potentially poisonous fish, head to **Tentake (天竹),** 6-16-6 Tsukiji (tel. 3541-3881), located on Harumi-dori next to a bridge. Although people who really know their fugu will tell you that the only time to eat it is from October through March, at Tentake you can enjoy fugu all year round. It's open from noon to 10pm and closed Sundays April through September and on the first and third Wednesday October through March. Finally, if seafood for breakfast or lunch just doesn't cut it, you might want to splurge at **Tamura (田村),** 2-12-11 Tsukiji (tel. 3541-2591), a modern kaiseki restaurant where the emphasis is on fresh seasonal vegetables. Choose one of the set lunches. Expensive but worth it, Tamura is open daily from noon to 2pm and 6 to 7:30pm (last order).

Leaving Tsukiji Market the same way you came and turning left after the entryway bridge, you will soon come back to Shin Ohashi-dori, where you should again turn left. Presently you will see the tall office headquarters of the:

7. **Asahi Shimbun,** one of the largest newspapers in Japan with a daily circulation of more than 7 million. The written dissemination of news in Japan began in the Edo Period, when tile blocks were distributed carrying such important news events as the destruction of Osaka Castle by Tokugawa forces in the 17th century and the suicide of the 47 masterless samurai in the early 18th century. The first Japanese-language newspaper was printed in 1862, while the first daily made its appearance in 1871. The *Asahi Shimbun* was established in Osaka in 1879, opening a Tokyo branch soon afterward. It wasn't until the great Kanto earthquake of 1923, however, that the Asahi got its big break in the Tokyo market. As Tokyo printing presses went down with the flames, the Osaka-based newspaper rushed out with detailed descriptions of the disaster, selling one million copies in one day. Incidentally, the Japanese must know at least

3,600 characters (called *kanji*) to read a Japanese newspaper, and yet adult literacy in Japan is estimated to be an astonishing 99%.

If you continue walking along this busy thoroughfare, in ten minutes or so you will come upon a stone bridge to the left with trees towering beyond. This marks the entrance to:

8. **Hama Rikyu Garden** (tel. 3541-0200), considered by some to be the best garden in Tokyo. Quiet and peaceful, especially on weekdays when it's practically deserted, it's certainly a welcome change after the frenetic activity of the Tsukiji Fish Market. Its origins can be traced back 300 years, when it served as a retreat for a former feudal lord and as duck-hunting grounds for the Tokugawa shoguns. In 1871 possession of the garden passed to the imperial family, who used it to entertain foreign dignitaries, including General Ulysses S. Grant who met with Emperor Meiji in the garden's tea house. After World War II, the garden was opened to the public. Come here to see how the upper classes enjoyed themselves during the Edo Period. Surrounded by water on three sides, it contains an inner tidal pool, spanned by three bridges draped with wisteria. There are also other ponds, a bird refuge, a promenade along the river lined with pine trees, moon-viewing pavilions, and teahouses. In a style popular during the Edo Period, the garden is laid out to utilize surrounding scenery in its composition, incorporating Mt. Fuji in its overall design. With Tokyo's tall buildings and smog, however, you'd be hard put to find Mt. Fuji nowadays. In fact, the beauty of the garden is somewhat spoiled by surrounding buildings, making it a real challenge to photograph any of the scenery without the 20th century looming in the background. The garden is open Tuesday through Sunday from 9am to 4:30pm (you must enter by 4pm).

☕ **Take a Break**   There are a couple of **open-air snack shops** in Hama Rikyu Garden selling drinks, ice cream, and other snacks. It's a great place to relax, refresh yourself, and enjoy the view.

You can walk from Hama Rikyu Garden to Shimbashi Station in about 10 minutes, but instead I strongly urge you to board one of the pleasure boats departing directly from inside Hama Rikyu Garden that will take you to Asakusa on the opposite end of Tokyo (see the next chapter for a recommended stroll through Asakusa). Ferries depart every hour or so, making their way along the Sumida River just as in past centuries boats carried wealthy townspeople to the pleasure district of Yoshiwara. Although most of what you see along the river today are the undersides of bridges and concrete embankments, I recommend the trip because it affords a different perspective of Tokyo—barges making their way down the river, high-rise apartment buildings with laundry fluttering from balconies, spanking new office buildings, warehouses, and superhighways. The boats pass under approximately a dozen bridges during the 40-minute trip, each bridge completely different and described in an English pamphlet.

If you're calling it quits and heading to the nearest station, Shimbashi Station, be sure to study the map at the exit of the garden that shows the route. Essentially, you should walk over the pedestrian bridge, cross busy Kaigandori and turn right and then keep to the left. After crossing Daiichikeihin, you'll see Shimbashi Station straight ahead. Once a renowned Geisha district, Shimbashi grew in importance when the nation's first train connected the station here with Yokohama in 1872. On the west side of the station is a 1945 steam locomotive commemorating the historic event.

Take a Break   One of Shimbashi's most well-known restaurants, **Hashizen,** 1-7-11 Shimbashi (tel. 3751-2700) has been selling tempura for more than 160 years. Especially popular among the lunch crowd is its *donburi,* with seafood placed on a bed of rice. Located on Sotobori-dori, it's open Monday to Saturday from 11:30am to 9pm and Sunday from noon to 8pm. Nearby is **Bee Hoon Azuma,** located on the second floor of the Shimbashi Ekimae Building right beside the station (tel. 3571-6078). This noodle shop boasts more than a dozen kinds of bee hoon dishes, Chinese noodles made of rice. Closed on Sunday, it's open for lunch Monday to Saturday from 11:30am to 2pm and for dinner Monday to Friday from 5 to 8pm.

ASAKUSA—OLD TOWN

Start: Hama Rikyu Garden (near Shimbashi Station); or Asakusa Station (exit 1 or 3).

Finish: Kappabashi-dori. Station: Tawaramachi.

Time: Allow approximately five hours, including the boat ride.

Best Times: Wednesday through Friday, when the crowds aren't as big.

Worst Times: Monday, when some attractions are closed, Tuesday, when the Drum Museum is closed, and Sunday, when shops on Kappabashi-dori are closed.

If anything remains of old Edo, Asakusa is it. This is where you'll find at least a remnant of the Japan of your fantasies—narrow streets with traditional wooden homes; old Japanese women in kimono, Tokyo's oldest and most popular temple, quaint shops selling boxwood combs, fans, sweet pastries, and other products of yore. For many Japanese, a visit to Asakusa is like stepping back to the days of their childhood.

Pleasure seekers have been flocking to Asakusa for centuries. Originating as a temple town back in the 7th century, it grew in popularity during the Tokugawa regime, as merchants grew wealthy and whole new forms of popular entertainment arose to cater to them. Theaters for Kabuki and Bunraku (puppet theater) flourished in Asakusa, as did restaurants and shops. By 1840, Asakusa had become Edo's main entertainment district, with various kinds of theaters, brothels, tea houses, and stalls selling everything from hair ornaments and sweets to medicine and beauty products. If you needed to replenish your supply of nightingale droppings (considered good for facial skin) or blackening agent for your teeth (a must for Edo beauties), you could do so at the shops of Asakusa. In stark contrast to the solemnity surrounding places of worship in the West, Asakusa's temple market had a carnival atmosphere reminiscent of medieval Europe, complete with street performers and exotic animals. It retains some of that festive atmosphere even today.

But Asakusa wasn't the only reason for a trip to this northern outpost of old Edo. Just a bit farther down the river was Yoshiwara, Edo's famous "floating world of pleasure." Opened in 1657 in the midst of rice fields far outside city gates, Yoshiwara served as Edo's licensed prostitution district. Surrounded by a moat and entered through a guarded gate, Yoshiwara had as many as 3,000 courtesans during its peak, some of whom had been sold into prostitution. To prevent them from fleeing, Yoshiwara's courtesans were allowed out of the compound only once a year during an autumn festival—a form of imprisonment that was abolished only in 1900. The services they rendered depended on how much their customers were willing to spend. Some men, so they say, stayed for days.

Today families, tour groups of retirees, and camera-toting tourists still flock to Asakusa, but their expectations are wildly different. World War II, which reduced much of the area to rubble, marked Asakusa's demise as Tokyo's main entertainment center, but pleasures in and around Asakusa still abound. With its Sensoji Temple, temple market, old-fashioned amusement park, shops, restaurants, and theaters, Asakusa still retains the charm of old downtown Edo more than anyplace else in Tokyo. If you had only one day to spend in Japan, this is the walking tour of Tokyo I'd most recommend.

• • • • • • • • • • • • • • • •

The most dramatic way to arrive in Asakusa is by boat. In the days of Edo, Asakusa was more than an hour's walk outside city gates, making a boat ride down the Sumida River the most popular way to travel to both Asakusa and

Yoshiwara. As Tokyo's largest river, Sumida flourished with life along its banks from the 17th to 19th centuries. Unfortunately, modern Tokyo has turned its back on its ancient waterways, encasing them with ugly concrete or simply filling them in. The only time the Sumida recaptures some of its past glory is during its annual summer fireworks display, begun in the mid-1600s. In addition, Sumida Park, extending north along the west bank of the river beginning at Asakusa, is lined with cherry trees and is particularly spectacular in spring. But even though the Sumida isn't what it used to be, a boat ride is still the most relaxing way to reach Asakusa and offers a view of Tokyo missed when riding the underground.

Therefore, I suggest you start this tour by heading first for Hama Rikyu Garden, located about a 10-minute walk from Shimbashi Station. Better yet, get up early in the morning and follow Walking Tour 3 of Tsukiji, which brings you to Hama Rikyu Garden at its conclusion. Ferries bound for Asakusa depart from the garden approximately every hour, arriving in Asakusa about 40 minutes later. If you wish to forgo the boat ride, take the Ginza line straight to Asakusa station.

Whether you travel by boat or subway, one of the first things you notice upon arrival in Asakusa is the Asahi Beer Hall on the opposite bank of the Sumida River. Designed by Philippe Starck, it's a squat building with a golden hops poised on top, looking all the world like a sperm about to dive into the Sumida River. The Asahi Beer Hall and its adjacent gold-colored office building contain several restaurants, good places to stop for lunch (see the Take a Break section later).

Walking inland on Kaminarimon-dori with your back toward the Sumida River, you will see almost immediately the colorful Kaminarimon Gate that marks the entrance to the temple. Across the street from this gate is the:

1. **Asakusa Information Center,** 2-18-9 Kaminarim on (tel. 3842-5566). Open daily from 9:30am to 8pm, it's staffed by English-speaking volunteers daily from 10am to 5pm. Stop here to pick up a map of the area and to ask directions to restaurants and other sights in the area you might be interested in visiting. An extra bonus is

its clean public restroom facilities. And that huge Seiko clock you see on its facade is a mechanical music clock, with performances every hour on the hour from 10am to 7pm.

It's now time to head across the street to the:

2. **Kaminarimon Gate,** unmistakable with its bright-red colors and 1,500-pound lantern hanging from the middle. Those statues inside the gate are the gods of wind to the right and thunder to the left, ready to protect the deity enshrined in the temple. The god of thunder is particularly fearsome—he has an insatiable appetite for navels. No doubt more than a few Japanese mothers have pointed out the scary god to their children, to encourage proper behavior on their visit to Asakusa. Such tactics must work, for I've never seen a Japanese child misbehave in public.

To the left of Kaminarimon Gate on the corner is:

3. **Tokiwado (常盤堂),** an open-air counter selling one of Asakusa's most popular souvenirs, *Ningyo-yaki* (a kind of sponge cake with a sweet bean-paste filling). In operation for more than 200 years, it's open daily from 9am to 9pm.

To the right of Kaminarimon Gate is another longstanding establishment:

4. **Kurodaya** (tel. 3844-7511), which opened its doors for business in 1856 and sells traditional Japanese papers, kites, papier-mâché masks, boxes, stationery, lanterns, dolls, and other products made of paper. It's open Tuesday through Sunday from 11am to 7pm.

Behind Kaminarimon Gate is a pedestrian lane called:

5. **Nakamise-dori,** which leads straight to the temple. Nakamise means "inside shops," and historical records show that vendors sold their wares here as early as the late 17th century. Today Nakamise-dori is lined on both sides with tiny stall after stall, many owned by the same family for generations, but if you're expecting austere religious offerings you're in for a surprise. You can buy fabrics, shoes, barking toy dogs, Japanese crackers (called *sembei*), trinkets, bags, umbrellas, Japanese dolls, fans, masks, and traditional Japanese accessories. How about a brightly colored straight hairpin? A black hairpiece? A wooden

Asakusa—Old Town

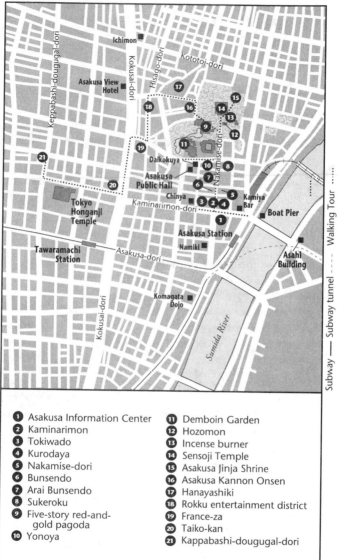

1. Asakusa Information Center
2. Kaminarimon
3. Tokiwado
4. Kurodaya
5. Nakamise-dori
6. Bunsendo
7. Arai Bunsendo
8. Sukeroku
9. Five-story red-and-gold pagoda
10. Yonoya
11. Demboin Garden
12. Hozomon
13. Incense burner
14. Sensoji Temple
15. Asakusa Jinja Shrine
16. Asakusa Kannon Onsen
17. Hanayashiki
18. Rokku entertainment district
19. France-za
20. Taiko-kan
21. Kappabashi-dougugal-dori

comb? A temporary tattoo in the shape of a dragon? It's a great place to shop for souvenirs, gifts, and items you have no earthly need for—a little bit of unabashed consumerism on the way to spiritual purification.

Among the many shops in the vicinity is:

6. **Bunsendo (文扇堂),** 1-30-1 Asakusa (tel. 3841-0077), a famous fan shop in business for more than a century and known for its special orders for Kabuki stars. To reach it, take the first left off of Nakamise-dori; Bunsendo is to the right on a corner and is open daily from 10:30am to 6pm. Its branch,

7. **Arai Bunsendo,** is located about halfway up Nakamise, on the left-hand side. On the right side of Nakamise-dori, the next to the last shop is:

8. **Sukeroku (助六),** (tel. 3844-0577), a truly unique shop filled with handmade miniature figures of traditional Japanese characters from mythological creatures to priests, farmers, entertainers, and animals, including the many castes from the Edo Period ranging from peasants to feudal lords. Some of the figures are quite expensive. In business since 1860, it's open every day except Thursday from 10am to 6pm.

After passing a kindergarten on your left (looking slightly out of place but a poignant reminder that this is still a residential neighborhood) and before reaching the second gate to the temple, you'll see a:

9. **five-story red-and-gold pagoda** to your left. It's a 1970 remake of one constructed during the time of the third shogun, Iemitsu, in the 17th century. Its top floor contains particles of Buddha's bones—or so the story goes. It seems every temple across Asia claims possession of one of Buddha's teeth or his bones.

And now comes the gem of this tour. Just a stone's throw from Nakamise-dori is one of Asakusa's treasures, a hidden garden, barely visible past the kindergarten. Most visitors to Asakusa pass it by, unaware of its existence, primarily because it isn't open to the general public. And yet, anyone can visit it simply by applying for permission from the monks who tend the grounds, which you can obtain by entering the small building to the left of the pagoda and walking straight down the corridor to the third door on the left. You'll be asked to sign your name and will be given a map showing the entrance to the garden, which is open daily from 9am to 3pm. However, because the garden is on the private grounds of the Demboin Monastery, it is occasionally closed due to functions. There's no way of telling until you get here whether you'll be able to see it, so you'll just have to trust to luck. Once you've obtained permission, retrace your steps down Nakamise past the kindergarten, and then turn right on Demboin-dori. While on this street, be sure to keep your eyes open for a unique shop on the left side:

10. **Yonoya,** 1-37-10 Asakusa (tel. 3844-1755), which specializes in boxwood combs. Its history stretches back 300 years, to a time when women's hairstyles were elaborate and complicated, as many woodblock prints testify. Today such handcrafted combs are a dying art, and some of the combs here cost more than $200. The shop is open every day except Wednesday from 10am to 7pm.

The second gate on the right-hand side of the street, across from the Asakusa Public Hall, marks the entrance to:

11. **Demboin Garden,** also spelled Dempoin Garden. If the gate is locked, ring the doorbell to be let in. Soon you will find yourself in a peaceful oasis in the midst of bustling Asakusa, in a countryside setting that centers on a pond filled with carp and turtles. It was designed in the 17th century by Enshu Kobori, a tea-ceremony master and famous landscape gardener who also designed a garden for the shogun's castle. Because most people are unaware that the garden exists or that they can see it, you may find yourself the sole visitor, making you feel like a privileged VIP. The best view is from the far side of the pond, where you can see the temple building and pagoda above the trees.

Take a Break As a major sightseeing destination in Tokyo, Asakusa boasts a myriad of dining opportunities. Just opposite the entrance to Demboin Garden, on the corner, is **Daikokuya (大黒家)**, 1-38-10 Asakusa (tel. 3844-1111), Asakusa's best-known restaurant for inexpensive tempura since 1887. A simple establishment, it's open every day except Wednesday from 11:30am to 8:30pm. **Chinya (ちんや)**, 1-3-4 Asakusa (tel. 3841-0010), located on Kaminarimon-dori just west of Kaminarimon Gate, has been serving sukiyaki and shabu-shabu since 1880. Moderately priced and now boasting a modern seven-story building (take off your shoes at the entrance), it's open Monday to Saturday from 11:45am to 9:15pm and Sunday and national holidays from 11:30am to 9pm. Also on Kaminarimon-Dori but this time east of Kaminarimon Gate is **Kamiya Bar,** 1-1-1 Asakusa (tel. 3841-5400), a casual restaurant founded in 1880 as one of Japan's first Western-style bars. Very much a place for the locals, it offers Western fare on its first and second floors and Japanese on the third. Order something from the plastic-food display cases. If you feel like a bracing drink, try Kamiya's own concoction, Denki-buran ("Electric Brandy"), which mixes vermouth, gin, wine, brandy, and curaçao. It's open from 11:30am to 9:30pm, closed on Tuesday.

If you take the road that leads straight south from Kaminarimon Gate with your back to Sensoji Temple, you will soon come to **Namiki (並木薮),** 2-11-9 Kaminarimon (tel. 3841-1340), an unassuming brown building on the right side with some bamboo trees by the front door. This one-room place with tatami and tables is Asakusa's best-known noodle shop and is open every day except Thursday from 11:30am to 7pm. Farther south down the street, past the Bank of Tokyo, is a large, old-fashioned restaurant on the right side of the street on a corner with blue curtains at its door. This is **Komagata Dojo (駒形どじょう),** 1-7-12 Komagata (tel. 3842-4001), an old-style dining hall specializing in *dojo,* a small freshwater eel. Seating is on the floor and waitresses are dressed in country-style clothes—a scene right out of the Edo Period. Indeed, this restaurant has been in business almost 200 years. Order the *yanagawa,* a mixture of egg, dojo, and vegetables, or dojo *nabe,* a stew of dojo cooked in front of you. If you really want your fill of dojo, order the *teishoku,* or set meal, which comes with several different variations of the river fish. The restaurant is open from 11am to 9pm daily.

Finally, there are several restaurants across the Sumida River worth the five-minute trek. On the 22nd floor of the Asahi Building are several dining establishments, all offering great views of Asakusa. Least expensive is the **Sky Room Asahi,** a coffee shop offering a limited menu of drinks open daily from 10am to 9pm. **La Ranarita** is a moderately priced Italian restaurant from Milan serving pizza, pasta, and seafood, while the more upscale **Restaurant Alaska** serves steaks and seafood. On the 21st floor is **Mochizuki,** a Japanese restaurant offering tempura, sashimi, shabu-shabu, and other dishes. Inside Philippe Starck's building is **La Flamme d'Or** with its—what can I say—rather stark interior. It offers very reasonably priced Western-style set lunches Monday through Friday, and of course, there's lots of Asahi beer. Restaurants in both buildings are open daily from 11:30am to 2pm and again from 5 to 10pm.

Return to Nakamise-dori and head north to the second gate:

12. **Hozo-Mon,** or Treasure-House Gate, built to house treasures of Sensoji Temple. It opens onto a square filled with pigeons and a large:

13. **incense burner,** where worshippers "wash" themselves to ward off or help against illness. If, for example, you have a sore throat, be sure to rub some of the smoke over your throat for good measure. But the dominating building of the square is:

14. **Sensoji Temple,** Tokyo's oldest and most popular temple. Founded in the 7th century and therefore already well established long before Tokugawa settled in Edo, Sensoji Temple is dedicated to Kannon, the Buddhist goddess of mercy, revered for her compassion for human weakness and her power to release humans from suffering. The temple is therefore popularly called Asakusa Kannon Temple. According to popular lore, the temple was founded more than 1,300 years ago after two fishermen netted the catch of their lives— a tiny golden statue of Kannon. A temple was built to enshrine it; word spread, and before long people flocked to Asakusa to worship it. Today the sacred statue is still housed in the temple, carefully preserved inside three boxes, but it's never presented to public view. That doesn't seem to bother the crowds of the faithful who flock to the temple to pay their respects and to seek favors of Kannon. The present building, made of ferroconcrete, was rebuilt after World War II from donations by the Japanese people.

Inside the temple's main building is a counter where you can buy your fortune by putting a 100-yen coin into a

Religion in Japan

The main religions in Japan are Shintoism, indigenous to Japan, and Buddhism, introduced to Japan in the 6th century. Although many Japanese believe in both faiths, neither plays a great influence in the everyday life of the Japanese. Unlike in the West, where churches have religious services daily or weekly, in Japan temples and shrines are generally visited for a specific purpose, primarily to give thanks or to ask for favors. On New Year's, for example, many Japanese throng to shrines to pray for good fortune in the coming year, while in summer they go to pay their respect to their ancestors. To the Japanese, religion is a way of thinking, a way of relating to one's world, environment, and family.

Shintoism evolved in ancient Japan in response to fears of demons and supernatural powers and is the worship of ancestors, national heroes, and all things in nature, both animate and inanimate, whether mountain, vegetable, star, or animal. Shintoism also embraces much of Confucianism, which entered Japan in the 5th century and stressed the importance of family and loyalty. There are no written doctrines or scriptures in Shintoism, nor is there an ordained code of morals or ethics.

The most important goddess in Shintoism is Amaterasu, the sun goddess, who is considered the progenitor of the Japanese imperial family. Central to the principles of Shintoism through the ages, therefore, was the deification of the emperor as a living god. Emperors held this revered position for more than 1,500 years, until the end of World War II, when former Emperor Hirohito was forced to renounce the claim to divinity and admit that he was an ordinary mortal just like everyone else. At this time, Shintoism also lost its official status as the national religion, a position it had held since the Meiji Restoration.

The place of worship in Shintoism is called a Jinja, or shrine. Every city, town, and hamlet has at least one shrine, and to most inhabitants it embodies the soul of their district. Tokyo's most famous shrine is Meiji Shrine in

Harajuku. The most obvious telltale sign of a shrine is its torii, an entrance gate, usually of wood, consisting of two tall poles topped with either one or two crossbeams. Sometimes there are several of these torii spread along the pathway leading to the shrine, reminding visitors that they are approaching a shrine and giving them time to achieve the proper frame of mind. Since purification and bodily cleanliness are greatly emphasized in Shintoism, Japanese will pause before a water trough just before the shrine to rinse out their mouths and wash their hands. At the shrine itself, worshippers will throw a few coins into a money box as a way to show gratitude or to ask for favors, clap their hands three times or ring a bell to get the attention of the gods, and then bow their heads and pray. Worshippers pray for good health, protection from harm, the safe delivery of a child, that sons get into good universities and daughters get good husbands, and anything else they may need. Certain shrines are auspicious for certain favors or conditions—some may be considered lucky for love, while others are good against certain ailments.

Buddhism was founded in India in the 5th century and was introduced to Japan via China and Korea in the 6th century, bringing with it the concept of eternal life. Buddhist places of worship are called temples, otera, and instead of a torii they will often have an entrance gate with a raised doorsill and heavy doors. Temples may also have a cemetery on their grounds, which Shinto shrines never have, and a pagoda. Tokyo's most famous temple is Sensoji Temple in Asakusa.

There are many different sects of Buddhism, but probably the most Japanese form of Buddhism is Zen Buddhism, which emphasizes a strictly disciplined lifestyle in the belief that it helps rid one of desire so that one can achieve enlightenment. There are no rites in Zen Buddhism, no dogmas, no theological conceptions of divinity. You do not analyze rationally but are supposed to know things intuitively. The strict and simple lifestyle of Zen appealed greatly to Japan's samurai warrior class, and many of Japan's arts, including the tea ceremony, arose from the practice of Zen.

wooden box and shaking it until a long bamboo stick emerges from a small hole. The stick will have a number on it, which corresponds to numbers on a set of drawers. Take out the fortune from the drawer which has your number. Although it's written only in Japanese, you can ask for a translation at the counter to the left (if the counter is un-occupied, you can also ask at the Asakusa Information Counter). But don't expect the translation to clear things up. My fortune contained such cryptic messages as "Getting a beautiful lady at your home, you want to try all people know about this" and "Stop to start a trip." If you find your fortune raises more questions than it answers or you simply don't like what it has to say, you can conveniently negate it by tying it to one of the wires provided or to the twig of a nearby tree, just another example of Japanese practicality.

If you walk around the temple to the right, on the north-east corner of the grounds is a small orange shrine:

15. **Asakusa Jinja Shrine,** built in commemoration of the two fishermen who found the statue of Kannon and the village headman who ordered the construction of the temple. It may seem strange to find a Buddhist temple and a Shinto shrine side by side, but in truth many Japanese consider themselves believers in both and find nothing unusual about incorporating two completely different religions into their lifestyle. Many Japanese, for example, are married in a Shinto ceremony, but when they die they'll almost certainly have a Buddhist funeral.

From Asakusa Jinja Shrine, walk west around the back side of Sensoji and then take the road that runs between Sensoji and the pagoda and follow it west, turning right at the shopping street. To the left is a brown ivy-covered building, the:

16. **Asakusa Kannon Onsen,** 2-7-26 Asakusa (tel. 3844-4141), one of Tokyo's most famous public baths and one of the few that boast water from a hot spring. In 1810 there were as many as 500 public bathhouses in Edo, not surprising when you consider that few homes had their own bathing facilities. Now that many Japanese can bathe at home, the neighborhood bath, or *sento,* has dwindled in popularity and number. Still, I suggest you visit a sento for

a real immersion in Japanese culture—but remember to soap up and rinse off completely before entering the bath, since Japanese use the same bath water (although Westerners may balk at the thought of using the same tub water, they usually don't think twice about jumping into a Jacuzzi at a health spa). You can find or buy everything you need at a public bathhouse—a small washcloth that doubles as a towel for drying off and even shampoo and underwear—so what are you waiting for? It's open every day except Thursday from 6:30am to 6pm.

Just to the north of the bathhouse is:

17. **Hanayashiki** (tel. 3842-8780), a rather corny amusement park that first opened in 1853 and still draws in the little ones. Small by today's comparisons, Tokyo's oldest amusement park offers a small roller coaster, carousel, and other diversions that appeal to youngsters and is open every day except Tuesday from 10am to 6pm (you must enter by 5:30pm).

Walk west past Hanayashiki in the direction of the towering Asakusa View Hotel. To your right you'll pass the Hisago-dori covered shopping street; immediately after Hisago-dori take the first left and walk straight. This is the:

18. **Rokku entertainment district,** all that remains of what was once a thriving nightlife district dating from the Meiji Period. Once the home of Kabuki theaters and tea houses, it now has pachinko parlors, cinemas, some theaters, light burlesque, and strip shows and is still popular among Tokyo's older working class. After two blocks you'll come to one of the most famous strip shows, located to the right on a corner:

19. **France-za,** 1-43-12 Asakusa (tel. 3841-6631). With four shows daily and open from 11:30am to 9pm, it leaves absolutely nothing to the imagination. Indeed, considering the rapt attention given the dancers by the businessmen (some of whom you half expect to pull out binoculars if not magnifying glasses), the shows themselves are almost like lessons in anatomy.

Turn right at France-za, cross the busy Kokusai-dori, and turn left. After a few blocks you will soon come to the:

20. **Taiko-kan** (Drum Museum), 2-1-1 Nishiasakusa (tel. 3842-5622), located opposite the Tower's Center Building. Actually, the ground floor is a shop selling drums and percussion instruments and items used in Japan's many festivals. The museum is up on the fourth floor and boasts a collection of more than 600 instruments, which are displayed on a rotating basis and include traditional Japanese drums as well as a variety of drums from all over the world. Most amazing is the fact that visitors can play most of the drums on display. The museum, which charges admission, is open Wednesday through Sunday from 10am to 5pm.

    Take a right out of the drum shop and then an immediate right again, heading west. After a few minutes you'll pass Tokyo Honganji Temple, and just past it, at the light, is:

21. **Kappabashi-dougugal-dori,** generally referred to simply as Kappabashi-dori. Turn right here, and you'll soon find yourself in Tokyo's foremost wholesale district for restaurant items. Pottery, chairs, tableware, cookingware, lacquerware, rice cookers, noren, and everything imaginable needed to run a restaurant is for sale here. Although the clientele is mostly restaurant owners, shops will sell to the general public, though they may require that purchases of bowls, plates, etc., be made in sets of five (by the way, you'll never find sets of four in Japan, since the number four sounds like the word for death and is therefore considered most unlucky). And yes, you can even buy those models of plastic food you've been drooling over in restaurant displays—mugs of foaming beer, ice cream, fish, sushi, pizza, spaghetti twirled around a fork suspended in the air. This is the place to buy that gift for the person who has everything. One of the best stores of this genre is the Sato Food Sample Company, down Kappabashi-dori to the right at 3-7I-4 Nishiasakusa (tel. 3844-1650). Like most stores here, it's open every day except Sunday and national holidays from 9:30am to 5:30pm.

    The nearest subway station is Tawaramachi, located on Asakusa-dori. From Kappabashi-dori, head south and then turn left on Asakusa-dori.

Take a Break If the plastic food displays of Kappabashi-dori look good enough to eat, it's probably time for some real food. A great place for lunch or to end the day is 28 floors above ground at the **Belvedere** (tel. 3847-1111) in the Asakusa View Hotel on Kokusai-dori. It serves a Western-style buffet lunch daily from noon to 2pm; tea time is from 2 to 4:30pm; and it reopens as a bar and cocktail lounge daily at 6pm. From here you have a bird's-eye-view of Sensoji Temple, the Asahi Beer Hall, Hanayashiki, Demboin Garden, and everywhere else you've walked today. Another good place to end the day is **Ichimon** (一文), 3-12-6 Asakusa, located northeast of the Kokusai-dori and Kototoi-dori intersection. Decorated like an old farmhouse, it specializes in sake and has a unique system in which customers buy mon, wooden tokens, which are traded for food and drinks. It's open Monday to Saturday from 5:30 to 10:30pm.

UENO SHITAMACHI

Start: South end of Ueno Park. Station: Ueno.

Finish: Ameya Yokocho flea market, along the tracks of the Yamanote Line. Station: Ueno or Okachimachi.

Time: Allow approximately five or six hours to see all the many sights in Ueno.

Best Times: Tuesday through Friday, when museums and shops aren't as crowded.

Worst Times: Monday, when the museums and zoo are closed.

Located on the northeast end of the Yamanote Line loop, Ueno is one of the most popular places in Tokyo with Japanese families on a day's outing. In contrast to the sophistication of the Ginza, Ueno has always been favored by the working class of Tokyo, even in the days of Edo, and together with Asakusa makes up the old Shitamachi, or old downtown. This is where merchants, craftsmen, and townspeople lived, worked, and played, and traces of their lives remain even today.

Ueno's main drawing card is Ueno Park, located atop a broad hill and famous throughout Japan for its cluster of historic monuments, zoo, and excellent museums, including the prestigious Tokyo National Museum. During the Edo Period, the park was the site of a vast temple complex, constructed in the 17th century as the private family temple and burial ground of the Tokugawa shoguns and therefore off limits to commoners. Called Kaneiji, the temple also served as protection from evil spirits and enemies that might attack Edo from the northeast, always considered by the Japanese as a city's most vulnerable boundary and therefore the easiest point of attack for invaders. The complex stretched over almost 300 acres, consisting of one main temple and 36 subsidiary temples. Unfortunately, most of the complex was destroyed in 1868, when 2,000 diehard shogun loyalists gathered on Ueno Hill for a last stand against the advancing forces of the imperial army. The defeat of the loyalists marked the end of the feudal the era and the opening of Japan to the West. In 1873, Ueno Park was opened to the public as one of the nation's first public parks.

● ● ● ● ● ● ● ● ● ● ● ● ● ● ● ●

Whether you arrive in Ueno by subway or the JR Yamanote Line, make your way to the main entrance of the Keisei Ueno Station (terminus of the Skyliner train from the Narita airport). There are many counters along the street here where you can buy sushi, sandwiches, and traditional obento (lunch boxes), in case you wish to pick up something for a picnic later in the park. At any rate, outside Keisei Ueno Station's main entrance are two steep flights of stairs leading up to an area of trees. This is the south entrance of:

1. **Ueno Park,** formerly the precincts of Kaneiji Temple. Although quite small compared to New York City's Central Park, this is Japan's largest city park and Tokyo's most important museum district, making it a favorite destination for families and school groups in search of culture, relaxation, and fun. It is also, by the way, a popular hangout for Tokyo's down-and-out homeless population, so don't be surprised to see them snoozing on benches and even living in the park's scattered sections of woods. With their possessions gathered neatly around them and their wet laundry spread out on bushes to dry, some of the homeless here actually look quite at home. Still, Japan's homeless are largely ignored by society, weird outcasts in a country where hard work and achievement are revered.

To the right at the top of the stairs as you enter Ueno Park is a bronze:

2. **statue of Takamori Saigo,** a samurai born in 1827 near Kagoshima on Kyushu Island. Rising through the ranks as a soldier and statesman, he was instrumental in helping restore the emperor to power after the downfall of the Tokugawa shogunate. He later, however, became disenchanted with the Meiji regime when the rights enjoyed by the samurai class, such as the right to wear swords, were suddenly rescinded. He led a revolt against the government that failed, and ended up taking his own life in ritual suicide. The statue was erected in the 1890s but later became the center of controversy when Gen. Douglas MacArthur, leader of the U.S. occupation forces in Japan after World War II, demanded that the statue be removed because of its emotional ties to nationalism. The Japanese people protested in a large public outcry and MacArthur finally relented. Today the statue, which depicts the stout Saigo dressed in a simple cotton kimono with his hand on his sword, is considered one of the three most famous statues in Japan (the Japanese, by the way, are fond of rating the best three of everything in the country, from the nation's three most beautiful sights to its three most beautiful bridges; their ratings, in my opinion, are clearly in the eyes of the beholder).

Ironically, behind the statue of Saigo and slightly to the left is a memorial dedicated to those very men Saigo opposed, the:

3. **tombs of the Shogitai Soldiers,** the diehard Tokugawa loyalists who resisted imperial forces on Ueno Hill in 1868. Of the several thousand loyalists who gathered here, considered masterless samurai because of the defiance they had shown in deserting their own feudal clans to fight for the shogun, 266 lost their lives. Tended by descendants of the soldiers, the grounds contain small paintings depicting the fierce battle.

Behind and to the left of the war memorial, on the other side of the pathway, is:

4. **Kiyomizu-do Kannon Temple,** completed in 1631 as a copy of the famous Kiyomizu Temple in Kyoto and one of the few buildings left standing after the battle of 1868.

Ueno Shitamachi

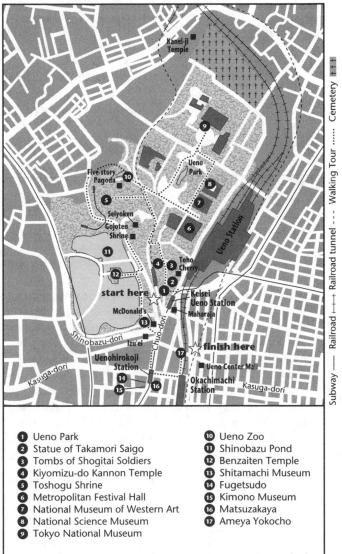

1. Ueno Park
2. Statue of Takamori Saigo
3. Tombs of Shogitai Soldiers
4. Kiyomizu-do Kannon Temple
5. Toshogu Shrine
6. Metropolitan Festival Hall
7. National Museum of Western Art
8. National Science Museum
9. Tokyo National Museum
10. Ueno Zoo
11. Shinobazu Pond
12. Benzaiten Temple
13. Shitamachi Museum
14. Fugetsudo
15. Kimono Museum
16. Matsuzakaya
17. Ameya Yokocho

Subway — Railroad ┼┼┼ Railroad tunnel --- Walking Tour ⋯⋯ Cemetery ┼┼┼

Unfortunately, extensive renovation work is expected to keep the temple under wraps until 1996, but a temporary worshipping hall has been set up in honor of the thousand-armed goddess enshrined here, protectoress of childbearing and child-raising. Women hoping to become pregnant come here to ask for the goddess's mercy; those whose wishes have been fulfilled return to pray for their child's good health and protection. Many worshippers leave behind a doll as a symbol of their child—you'll see some of those dolls here in the hall, some of which are very modern and look slightly out of place in the old temple. Once a year, a requiem service is held for all the dolls who have been brought to the temple, after which they are cremated in the temple's furnace. The temple rests on the crest of a hill, overlooking Shinobazu Pond.

Take a Break Located between Kiyomizu Temple and Toshogu Shrine, **Seiyoken** (tel. 3821-2181) opened in 1876 as one of Japan's first restaurants serving Western food. Now a nondescript building dating from the 1950s, it nonetheless is the best place to eat in Ueno Park and serves pricey but quite good classic French cuisine, with a relaxing view of greenery outside its large windows. It's open daily from 11am to 8pm, with reasonably priced set lunches offered to 2pm. In the same building is an inexpensive dining hall, good for snacks, fast food, and drinks. If it's fine weather, I suggest you head for **Toho Cherry** (tel. 3836-4375), an informal restaurant with a beer garden located in the south end of Ueno Park just a stone's throw from the statue of Saigo Takamori. Open every day except Monday from 11am to 8pm, it offers shabu-shabu, curry rice, hamburgers, and other simple dishes. Throughout Ueno Park are also small kiosks and huts selling drinks, snacks, and ice cream.

Walking north from Kiyomizu Temple, you will soon pass orange torii (made, horrendously enough, out of plastic!) and Seiyoken restaurant on your left. Following signs that say "Ueno Zoo," turn left at the Lions Club totem pole. Soon, to your left, you will see the stone torii that marks the entrance to:

5. **Toshogu Shrine,** Ueno Park's most famous religious structure and dedicated to Ieyasu Tokugawa, founder of the Tokugawa Shogunate. Stop here to pay respects to the man who made Edo the seat of his government and thus elevated the small village to the most important city in the country.

Actually, the shrine here is just one of many shrines through-out the country built in honor of Ieyasu, with the one in Nikko being the most famous as the final resting place of Ieyasu himself. Like Nikko's Toshogu Shrine, this one was erected by Ieyasu's grandson, Iemitsu, and is also joyously colorful with brilliant reds, blues, greens and gold orna-mentation. Completed in 1651, it remarkably survived the civil war of 1868, the Great Kanto Earthquake of 1923, and even World War II. The pathway leading to the shrine is lined with massive stone lanterns, as well as 50 copper lanterns donated by daimyo (feudal lords) from all over Japan and used for purification fires during religious ceremonies. To the right of the pathway is a five-storied pagoda (located on zoo grounds), covered entirely in lac-quer and constructed in 1639. Also on the temple grounds is the charred remains of a tree discovered in nearby Nishi-Nippori in 1991, burned during bombing raids of 1945 and placed here as an appeal for peace. Near it are photo-graphs of the war's destruction in Hiroshima and Nagasaki. The entrance to the shrine itself is to the left, open daily from 9am to 6pm in summer, 4:30pm in winter. I heartily recommend you pay the small admission fee required here, since it allows you to see the exquisite art work inside the shrine itself, including murals by a famous Edo artist, Kano Tan-yu, and samurai armor worn by Ieyasu. On a light note, you'll also see signs admonishing you to refrain from mak-ing bonfires, just in case you were contemplating a cookout on these sacred grounds.

Across from Toshogu Shrine is a miniature amusement park for children with a half dozen rides. Walk through it or around it to Ueno Park's main square, marked by an art-ificial pond with a fountain in the middle. Keep walking straight, past the pigeons, people feeding the pigeons, and the koban police box. That building to your right is the:

6. **Metropolitan Festival Hall,** opened in 1961 as a venue for classical music concerts, ballet, and dance. The build-ing to the left is the:

7. **National Museum of Western Art** (Kokuritsu Seiyo Bijutsukan, tel. 3828-5131), built in 1959 with a main building designed by French architect Le Corbusier. As its

name signifies, it features Western art, with a concentration of works from the 19th century, mainly French impressionism. Though there are far better collections in Europe, it does include works by Monet, Sisley, Manet, Delacroix, Gauguin, Courbet, Cézanne, Degas, El Greco, and Goya. The museum is perhaps most famous for its 50-some sculptures by Rodin, cast by his original molds and comprising the third-largest Rodin collection in the world. There are also special exhibits, for which an additional admission is charged. Note that part of the museum's collections are closed due to renovations, with an expected reopening in 1997. It's open every day except Monday from

Cherry Blossom Season

If you come to Ueno during that brief single week in April when the cherry blossoms burst forth, consider yourself lucky. Cherry blossoms have always been dear to the Japanese heart as a symbol of beauty, fragility, and the transitory nature of life itself, and with Ueno Park's hundreds of cherry trees, the Japanese flock en masse here to celebrate the birth of spring. It's not, however, the spiritual communion with nature that you might think.

If ever there was an excuse to get rowdy and drunk, the cherry blossom season is it. Employees of every company in Tokyo, it seems, converge on Ueno Park, Sumida Park, and other parks known for their cherry trees to shed themselves of their winter shells and with them their inhibitions. Each company marks its territory on the asphalt walkways with plastic tarps or cardboard, so that by evening there's hardly a place left to sit down. Everyone eats and drinks, some dance, and far too many display their talents or lack thereof with karaoke, singing loudly into microphones. The more everyone drinks, the friendlier they get. If you're a foreigner, chances are you'll be invited to sit down and join them—and by all means do. You'll all sit there drinking and being merry, seemingly oblivious to the pink and fragile blossoms shimmering above.

9:30am to 5pm (remember, you must enter museums at least a half hour before closing times).

Just past the art museum to the north is a building with a locomotive outside, the:

8. **National Science Museum** (Kokuritsu Kagaku Hakubutsukan, tel. 3822-0111 or 3822-0114). This sprawling complex, comprising four color-coded buildings with a fifth one under construction, covers everything from the evolution of life to electronics in Japan. Unfortunately most displays are in Japanese (be sure to pick up the museum's English pamphlet), but the museum is worth visiting for its displays relating to Japan. There are also plenty of exhibits geared to children. Dinosaurs greet visitors on the ground floor of the main hall, while up on the third floor plants and animals of Japan are featured, including marine life such as huge king crabs, the Japanese brown bear, the Japanese crested ibis, and the Japanese monkey. Also on the third floor is a small collection of clocks, including Japanese clocks that used temporal hours rather than chronometric time as used in Europe.

Other highlights include its displays on the origin and development of the Japanese people, a hands-on discovery room for children, a flight simulator, a Zero fighter plane used in World War II, and a short film featuring 18 models of lifelike dinosaurs. Among my favorites are the map of Japan showing the location of all its active volcanoes, hot springs, and sites of major earthquakes (quite an impressive sight and one that drives home the fact that Japanese have lived with the threat of natural disasters throughout their history), and the stuffed hide of Hachiko on the second floor of the Green Hall, an Akita who gained everlasting fame for its loyalty to its dead master and immortalized with a statue at Shibuya Station. There's also a room devoted to traditional technology in Japan, with demonstrations showing the making of Japanese paper and silk, the weaving and dying of textiles, and the manufacture of lacquer (did you know, for example, that lacquer comes from the sap of the lac tree?). The Science Museum is open from 9am to 4:30pm, closed on Mondays.

Take a right out of the Science Museum and a left at the road, which quickly brings us to Tokyo's most famous museum, the:

9. **Tokyo National Museum** (Tokyo Kokuritsu Hakubutsukan, tel. 3822-1111). If you go to only one museum during your stay in Japan, this should be it. Not only is it Japan's largest and oldest museum, it's also the largest repository of Japanese art in the world. This is the place to go to see antiques from Japan's past—old kimono, samurai armor, priceless swords, lacquerware, pottery, porcelain, scrolls, screens, calligraphy, ancient burial objects, ornamental roof tiles, ukiyo-e (woodblock prints), and more. Altogether the museum has about almost 90,000 items in its collections, including more than 10,000 paintings, 1,000 sculptures, 15,500 metalworks, 3,000 swords, 3,700 pieces of lacquerware, 27,000 archeological finds, and 7,500 works of foreign Eastern art. Needless to say, its collections are too vast to display all at once, so they're changed on a rotating basis. No matter how many times you visit the museum, therefore, you'll always see different things.

The museum encompasses three main buildings, with an additional one slated for opening by the turn of the century. The Main Gallery, straight ahead as you enter the main gate, is the most important, containing Buddhist sculptures, armor and helmets, woodblock prints, lacquerware, swords, textiles, ceramics from prehistoric times, paintings, calligraphy, and scrolls. The Toyokan is the Gallery of Eastern Antiquities and houses archeological artifacts from Asian countries outside Japan: Egyptian relics, stone reliefs from Cambodia, embroidered wall hangings and textiles from India, Korean bronze and celadon, Buddhas from Pakistan, Thai and Vietnamese ceramics, and Chinese art, including jade, glass, stone reliefs, paintings, calligraphy, mirrors, lacquerware, ceramics, and bronzes. The Hyokeikan Gallery contains archeological relics of Japan, including pottery and objects recovered from ancient burial mounds. One room is devoted to items once used in daily life by the Ainu, an indigenous ethnic group native to Japan's northern island of Hokkaido. Closed on Monday, the museum is open the rest of the week from 9am to 4:30pm.

From the National Museum, walk straight ahead (south) to the artificial pond with the dancing fountain. Watch how the fountain changes, bubbling with small eruptions and then bursting forth high into the air. Walking around the fountain to the right, turn right after passing the clock in the square, following signs to the:

10. **Ueno Zoo** (Ueno Dobutsuen, tel. 3828-5171). Open every day except Monday from 9:30am to 4:30pm, it was founded in 1882 and is Japan's oldest zoo. It seems rather small by today's standards and I can't help but feel sorry for the confined space of some of the animals, but Ueno Zoo remains one of the most well-known zoos in Japan, due in part to its giant pandas, donated by the Chinese government to mark the re-establishment of diplomatic relations between the two countries following World War II. These celebrities are so popular that there are always long lines to their cages on weekends, and the souvenirs you can buy with pandas on them seem endless. There are also Japanese macaques, polar bears, California sea lions, penguins, gorillas, giraffes, zebras, elephants, deer, and tigers. Be sure, too, to see the five-storied pagoda mentioned earlier in the walk. The zoo consists of two parts, connected via a monorail and a footbridge. End your tour of the zoo at:

11. **Shinobazu Pond** (you can also get to Shinobazu Pond without entering the zoo by retracing your steps to those orange plastic torii and walking downhill toward the pond, passing the Gojoten Shrine along the way). This marshy pond was constructed in the 17th century so that visitors to the various shrines in the area had a nice view of water on which to rest their eyes. Teahouses used to line the pond's banks. Now part of the pond has literally gone to the birds: It's a sanctuary for cormorants, still used for fishing in some parts of Japan (cormorants are good underwater swimmers, but to prevent them from swallowing what they catch, rings are fastened around their necks). The pond is filled with lotus plants, a lovely sight when they bloom in August.

Exit Ueno Zoo via the Benten Gate, located at the southeastern edge of Shinobazu Pond. Keep walking straight, till presently you will see an island in the middle of the pond, connected to the bank with a walkway and home of the:

12. **Benzaiten Temple.** It's dedicated to the goddess of fortune, so you certainly don't want to pass it by.

Take a right out of the temple, walking past the children's playground on the left, and soon to your left you'll see the:

13. **Shitamachi Museum** (Shitamachi Fuzoku Shiryokan, tel. 3823-7451). *Shitamachi* means "downtown" and refers to the area of Tokyo where commoners used to live, mainly around Ueno and Asakusa. There's very little left of old downtown Tokyo, and with that in mind this museum seeks to preserve for future generations a way of life that was virtually wiped out by the Great Kanto Earthquake of 1923, World War II, and modernization. On the ground floor are shops and homes set up as they may have looked back then, showing how the people lived and worked and including a merchant's shop and a candy shop, as well as a Shitamachi tenement house that was common at the turn of the century. A long narrow building with one roof over a series of dwelling units separated by thin wooden walls, these were the homes of the poorer people, confined to narrow back alleys. Everyone knew everyone else's business—few secrets could be kept in such crowded conditions as these. The alleyways served as common living rooms. Children played in them and families sat outside to catch whatever breeze there might be. The museum is filled with the utensils, furniture, and objects of everyday life, all donated by people living in Shitamachi. Note the bamboo basket suspended from the ceiling of the merchant's shop—it was used to transport personal belongings as families fled their homes during the city's frequent fires. On the second floor of the museum are more items used in daily life, including children's games, kitchen utensils, clothing, and tools, most of which are not behind glass but are simply lying around so that you can pick them up and examine them more closely. The museum, often noisy with visiting school groups, is open every day except Monday from 9:30am to 4:30pm.

Take a left out of the museum, a left at the street, a right at the stoplight and then head south on Chuo-dori. Across from Matsuzakaya, on the right, is:

14. **Fugetsudo (風月堂),** 1-20-10 Ueno (tel. 3831-1111), a pastry and coffee shop famous for its sponge cake. It's so popular with Japanese women that you probably won't find a seat in its first- or fourth-floor coffee shops, so console yourself with a small purchase of cake to eat later in your hotel room, or perhaps even for tomorrow's breakfast. It's open daily from 11am to 9:30pm.

Just past Fugetsudo in the next building to the right is the:

15. **Kimono Museum,** 1-20-11 Ueno (tel. 3839-8620), located up on the seventh floor. Its single showroom is dedicated to the kimono, which has changed little since its creation in the 8th century and still uses a sash (called an *obi*) rather than buttons or fasteners to keep it closed. The museum changes its displays every month, with themes ranging from modern designs to those used in Kabuki theater or everyday life. It's open every day except Tuesday from 11am to 5pm.

Across the street is the:

16. **Matsuzakaya department store,** 3-29-5 Ueno (tel. 3832-1111), which consists of two buildings and contains the usual departments for food, clothing, electronics, and accessories. It's open every day except Wednesday from 10am to 7pm.

Walk past the department store on Kasuga-dori toward the elevated platform of Okachimachi Station, passing Ueno Center Mall, a shopping lane lined with small boutiques. The next street to the left, just before the overhead tracks, is:

17. **Ameya Yokocho,** a narrow pedestrian shopping street along the west side of, as well as under, the elevated tracks of the Yamanote Line between Ueno and Okachimachi Stations. Originally it served as a wholesale market for candy and snacks (Ameya means candy store and Yokocho means narrow lane) and after World War II as a black market in U.S. army goods (some contend that the "Ame" stems from an abbreviation of American). Today Ameya Yokocho (also shortened to Ameyacho or Ameyoko) consists of hundreds

of stalls and shops selling at a discount everything from fish and vegetables to clothing and handbags. Housewives shop here for fresh cuts of tuna, squid, crab, fish eggs, eel, seaweed, pistachios, fruits, and vegetables, while Tokyo's youth come here for costume jewelry, cosmetics, socks, jackets, jeans, hosiery, watches, bags, clothing, and sporting goods. It's most crowded in the early evening, as workers rush through on their way home. Some shops close Wednesday, but otherwise most are open daily from about 10am to 7 or 8pm.

The closest stations are right overhead on the Yamanote Line—Ueno and Okachimachi.

Take a Break   There are several bars, coffee shops, and restaurants around the Ameya Yokocho area. For a specific recommendation, across from the Shitamachi Museum, next to Kentucky Fried Chicken, is **Izu'ei (伊豆栄),** 2-12-22 Ueno (tel. 3831-0954), a modern restaurant that has served eel since the Edo Period and boasts its own charcoal furnace in the mountains (the charcoal used in grilling eel is considered one of the most important factors in the taste of the eel itself). Choose from the plastic-display case outdoors or from a pamphlet with pictures, or order the unagi donburi, rice with strips of eel on top. It's open daily from 11am to 9:30pm. If Indian food is more to your taste, head for **Maharaja,** located on the third floor of the Nagafuji Building Annex at 4-9-6 Ueno (tel. 3835-0818), which is a shiny white building between Chuo-dori and the Ameya Yokocho shopping street. It's open daily from 11am to 10pm.

HARAJUKU & AOYAMA— TOKYO TRENDSETTERS

Start: Japan Traditional Craft Center, Aoyama-dori and Gaien-Nishi-dori intersection. Station: Gaienmae, then exit 1a at the south (*minami*) end of the station

Finish: Yoyogi Park. Station: Harajuku.

Time: Allow approximately six or seven hours, including stops along the way.

Best Times: Sunday, when you can relax over a Sunday brunch and when Omotesando-dori becomes a pedestrian zone and dancers converge on the scene. If you want to have brunch, I suggest you set out on this walk by 10am.

Worst Times: On Monday and from the 27th to the end of every month, when the Ota Memorial Museum of Art is closed; on Thursday, when the Oriental Bazaar and Japan Traditional Craft Center are closed.

Harajuku is one of my favorite neighborhoods in Tokyo. Sure, I'm too old to really fit in. Anyone older than 25 is apt to feel ancient here, for this is Tokyo's most popular and trendy hangout for Japanese high-school and college students. But I like Harajuku for its vibrancy, its side-walk cafés and international restaurants, its street vendors, its fashionable clothing boutiques, and the endless parade of Tokyo's self-conscious youth. Harajuku is where the young come to see and be seen—Japanese punks, girls dressed in black, and young couples in their fashionable best. Harajuku and neighboring Aoyama are also home of Tokyo's most venerable Shinto shrine, an excellent woodblock-print museum, Tokyo's best-known souvenir shop, a store selling exquisite hand-crafted traditional items, a museum of Asian art surrounded by a peaceful garden, and a park with wide-open spaces. Formerly the training grounds of the Japanese army and later the residential area of American families during the Occupation, Harajuku was also the site of the 1964 Olympic Village. With its cosmopolitan atmosphere, it's a popular destination also for the growing number of young foreigners working in Tokyo.

If at all possible, come to Harajuku on a Sunday, when spending an afternoon here is like going to a local carnival. There are gawkers and hawkers, performers and spectators, the dull and the outrageous. There's dancing in the street, flea markets, and crowds, crowds, crowds, but, as at the local fair, no one seems to mind. I have my suspicions that for many of the Japanese, being part of the crowd is exactly why they come.

• • • • • • • • • • • • • • • •

From Gaienmae Station, walk south about three minutes on Aoyama-dori in the direction of the towering Bell Commons building. On the corner of Aoyama-dori and Gaien-Nishi-dori, above the Häagen-Dazs ice-cream parlor, is the:

1. **Japan Traditional Craft Center,** located on the second floor of the Plaza 246 Building at 3-1-1 Minami Aoyama (tel. 3403-2460) with an entrance on Aoyama-dori. Established to publicize and distribute information on Japanese crafts, this lovely shop is devoted to beautifully crafted traditional items and is well worth a visit even if you can't afford to buy anything. In addition to its permanent exhibition, it sells various handmade crafts from all over Japan that are changed on a regular basis and usually

include lacquerware, ceramics, fabrics, paper products, metalwork, some furniture, and more. Bamboo baskets, knives, cast-iron tea pots, boxes made from cherry bark, chopsticks, lacquered trays, stone lanterns, and fans are just some of the exquisitely crafted items you may find here. Prices are high but rightfully so. In a corner is a video screen where you can watch videos showing the making of Japanese swords, textiles, bamboo ware, woodblock prints, and other traditional crafts. The store is open every day except Thursday from 10am to 6pm.

Take a left out of the craft center and continue walking south on Aoyama-dori. This avenue is the center of Aoyama, one of Tokyo's trendiest addresses. Chic and upscale, it's a yuppified version of neighboring Harajuku and boasts a remarkable number of designer boutiques, fashionable restaurants, and well-heeled customers. After about five minutes you'll reach Omotesando-dori, Harajuku's main boulevard and marked by two huge stone lanterns. Turn left here, where you'll find a handful of designer shops. First comes:

2. **Issey Miyake** on the left at 3-18-11 Minami-Aoyama (tel. 3423-1407), open daily from 11am to 8pm and selling both men's and women's fashions. Now well known both at home and abroad, Miyake was one of many Japanese who first had to go abroad to make a name for himself before the Japanese took notice. His clothes are rich in texture and fabrics.

To the right is:

3. **Comme des Garçons,** 5-2-1 Minami-Aoyama (tel. 3406-3951), the showcase of Rei Kawakubo's designs for both men and women. Kawakubo is one of my favorite Japanese designers and one of the few females in the business. Her line of Comme des Garçons consists of loose-fitting, unusually cut clothing that is often black, off-white, or plain neutral. This shop is also open daily from 11am to 8pm.

Farther down the street, past Yoku Moku coffee shop (see "Take a Break" below) on the right, is:

4. **Yohji Yamamoto,** 5-3-6 Minami-Aoyama (tel. 3409-6006), open from 11am to 8pm daily. As with all Yohji

Harajuku & Aoyama

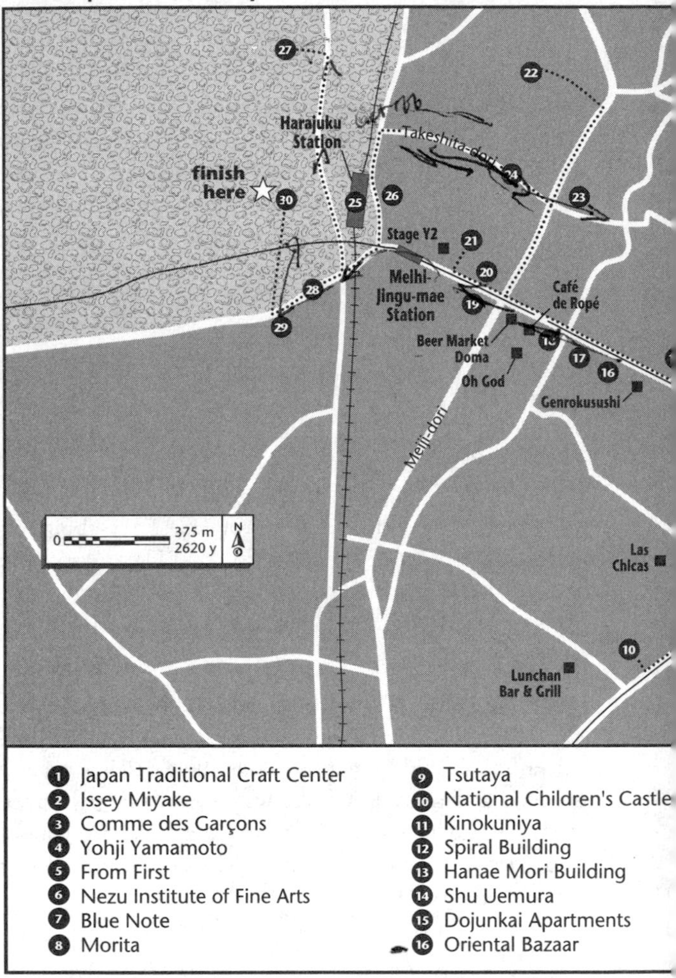

Harajuku Station
finish here
Takeshita-dori
Stage Y2
Meiji-Jingu-mae Station
Café de Ropé
Beer Market Doma
Oh God
Genrokusushi
Meiji-dori
0 375 m 2620 y
N
Las Chicas
Lunchan Bar & Grill
1 Japan Traditional Craft Center
2 Issey Miyake
3 Comme des Garçons
4 Yohji Yamamoto
5 From First
6 Nezu Institute of Fine Arts
7 Blue Note
8 Morita
9 Tsutaya
10 National Children's Castle
11 Kinokuniya
12 Spiral Building
13 Hanae Mori Building
14 Shu Uemura
15 Dojunkai Apartments
16 Oriental Bazaar

9700

Yamamoto shops, it has an interesting avant-garde interior that reminds me of the inside of a mine, or perhaps the underbelly of a railroad trestle, or . . . who knows?

Just past it, also on the right, is the brick:

5. **From First building,** with concessions for Cerruti 1881 for women, Salvatore Ferragamo, Issey Miyake and others, most open daily from 11am to 8pm.

Continue walking in the same direction, curving to the left, until you come to a stoplight. Cross the street and turn right, following the sign that directs you to the:

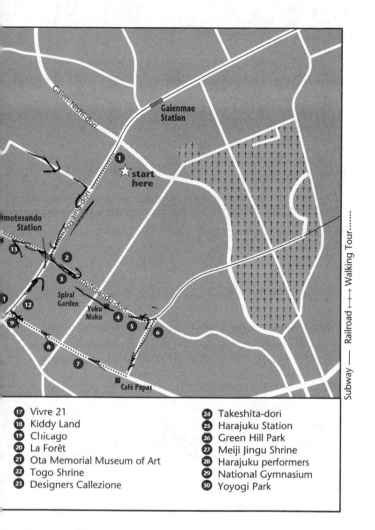

Subway —— Railroad ┼─┼ Walking Tour·······

6. Nezu Institute of Fine Arts, 6-5-1 Minami-Aoyama (tel. 3400-2536). One of Tokyo's best private museums, it houses a fine collection of Asian art, including Chinese bronzes, Japanese calligraphy, Korean ceramics, and other artwork ranging from paintings and sculpture to lacquerware and Buddhist art. Among its works are two famous paintings, the 13th-century "Nachi Waterfall" from the Kamakura Period and irises stenciled on gold by Ogata Korin from the Edo Period. In addition to its permanent displays, special exhibitions highlight specific art such as antique Imari ware, Buddha statues, or decorative Chinese clocks. Although admission to the museum is rather high compared to other art museums, its price includes entrance to a small garden with several teahouses. During my last visit, kimono-clad women were making their way along the sun-dappled pathways to one of the teahouses, in a timeless scene that could have been from a century ago. The museum is open every day except Monday from 9:30am to 4:30pm (you must enter by 4pm).

Take a Break Between Comme des Garçons and Yohji Yamamoto is a great place to rest weary feet. Called **Yoku Moku** and located in a blue-tiled building at 5-3-3 Minami-Aoyama (tel. 5485-3340), it's a cheerful coffee shop with seating both indoors and outdoors and offering ice cream, sherbet, and wonderful desserts, all scrumptiously depicted in an illustrated menu. It's open daily from 10am to 7pm. On the grounds of the Nezu Institute of the Arts is the **Café Gazebo,** which offers a view of the garden with drinks, cake, and coffee. Not far from the Nezu museum is **Café Papas,** 6-11-1 Minami-Aoyama (tel. 3400-0884), owned by fashion biggies Bigi Co. and decorated like a New England boathouse with comfortable booths. In addition to its beer, coffee, espresso, cappuccino, cake, and ice cream, it offers a limited menu of salad, pizza, spaghetti, and sandwiches for lunch and dinner (on weekends, only sandwiches are served at lunch). Opening daily at 11:30am, it closes at 10pm Monday to Friday, at 9pm Saturday, and 8pm Sunday.

Take a left out of the Nezu Institute of Fine Arts and walk straight to the T-intersection with a stoplight. Straight ahead is Café Papas, described above. Take a right here, onto what is known locally as Antique-dori. There used to be a number of antique stores along this street, but in recent years the number of antique shops have dwindled and given way to fashion boutiques, among them Hugo Boss and Nino Cerruti. There aren't many nightlife options in this neck of the woods, but about halfway down the street on the left side is:

7. Blue Note, 5-13-3 Minami-Aoyama (tel. 34-7-5781), testimony to the popularity of jazz in Japan. Cousin to the famous Blue Note in New York and almost an exact replica with its interior of blue, this sophisticated club draws top-notch American musicians at yen-inflated prices.

Farther down the street, also on the left, is one of the few remaining antique shops:

8. **Morita,** 5-12-2 Minami-Aoyama (tel. 3407-4466), which specializes in folkcrafts and textiles, including material taken from antique kimono. It's open Monday to Saturday from 10am to 7pm and Sunday and holidays from 10am to 6pm.

Near the end of the street on the left side is:

9. **Tsutaya (つたや),** 5-10-5 Minami-Aoyama (tel. 3400-3815), which, as its sign says, carries "All Necessaries for Ikebana and Tea Ceremony." For ikebana (flower arranging) it has hundreds of vases, bamboo baskets, mats, and platforms for displaying flowers, scissors, and accessories. It's open from 9:30am to 6:30pm, closed the first and fourth Sunday of every month.

The intersection just past this shop brings you back to Aoyama-dori. If you have kids in tow, you might want to cross the street and turn left. Within five minutes you'll see to your right the:

10. **National Children's Castle** (Kodomo no Shiro), 5-53-1 Jingumae (tel. 3797-5666), an indoor playground designed to appeal to children of all ages and featuring various rooms devoted to different activities. The Play Hall contains building blocks, a jungle gym, table tennis, a large doll house, and computer games, while the art room is staffed with instructors who help children with projects commensurate to their ages. A video room with private cubicles allows viewers to make selections from a stocked library of English and Japanese videos, including fairy tales, the "Golden Book" series, "Sesame Street," and rock videos. On the roof is an outdoor playground. Admission is charged, and it's open Tuesday to Friday from 12:30 to 5:30pm, and Saturdays, Sundays, and holidays from 10am to 5:30pm.

Take a Break If it's Sunday and you want brunch, you're in luck. Harajuku and Aoyama offer more choices for Sunday brunch than anywhere else in Tokyo, which also means that they attract a large foreign clientele. To be safe, make reservations beforehand, since these places are popular. Located on the fifth floor of the Hanae Mori Building on Omotesando-dori (described in more detail below), **L'Orangerie de Paris,** 3-6-1 Kita-Aoyama (tel. 3407-7461) is popular with Tokyo's well-heeled foreign population and is the most expensive and exclusive brunch spot in the area. It is open for Sunday brunch from 11am to 2:30pm; otherwise, set lunches are offered Monday to Saturday from 11:30am to 2:30pm. Slightly cheaper and more casual is **Spiral Garden** in the Spiral Building on Aoyama-dori, which serves a Sunday brunch from 11am to 2pm which includes an appetizer buffet with an array of egg dishes, pasta, soup, salads, and desserts. On a side street south of the National Children's Castle is **Lunchan Bar & Grill,** 1-2-5 Shibuya (tel. 5466-1398), a cheerful and airy American-style restaurant with large windows and jazz playing softly in the background. Sunday brunch, served from 11am to 3pm, includes a glass of champagne, mimosa, or bloody Mary and a choice of entrée ranging from eggs benedict to omelets and pancakes. Otherwise, the regular menu, available Monday to Saturday from 11:30am to 11pm and on Sunday from 3 to 10pm, includes pizza, sandwiches, pasta, and seafood at reasonable prices. **Las Chicas,** 5-47-6 Jingumae (tel. 3407-6865), is tucked away on a small side street that runs beside Citibank from Aoyama-dori. Opened by fashion house Vision Network, Las Chicas is part of a small complex that includes a fashion boutique, a CD store carrying Reggae, Sha, Latin music, jazz, funk, and New Age music, a hair salon, and restaurant, café, and bar with pleasant seating on an outdoor terrace. A foreign staff (more than a few of whom are aspiring models) and an eclectic menu that combines ingredients from both East and West draws foreigners, many in the fashion and design field, who come for hearty portions of a changing menu that may include roast lamb with a spinach and cream sauce, salmon steak with herbs and pumpkin, or chick pea curry. Las Chicas is open Monday to Friday from 11am to 10:30pm and on weekends from 9:30am to 10:30pm. If all you want is a quick and cheap cup of coffee and a sandwich or pastry, there's a Pronto coffeeshop on Aoyama-dori at

3-12-7 Kita-Aoyama (tel. 5485-3129), open daily from 7:30am to 11pm.

Heading back north on Aoyama-dori, past Pronto on your left is:

11. **Kinokuniya,** 3-11-7 Kita-Aoyama (tel. 3409-1231), which began as a small produce stand and then expanded into Japan's first western-style supermarket in 1953. It's still one of the best places in town to shop for western and international groceries and a real lifesaver for Tokyo's foreign population. If you've ever walked away with a carton of soy drink when you meant to purchase milk, you'll know what I mean. Campbell's soup, pancake mix, Mexican foodstuffs, cheddar cheese, wines, and more—all with labels you can actually read—are sold here daily from 9:30am to 8pm.

Farther north and on the other side of the street is the:

12. **Spiral Building,** 5-6-23 Minami Aoyama, which contains the Spiral Garden café on its ground floor, a spacious exhibition space, a Thai restaurant, and, my favorite, Spiral Market up on the second floor. Open daily from 11am to 8pm, this shop contains a wonderful selection of modern kitchen and household items, including tableware and utensils, as well as gifts ranging from jewelry and mobiles to stationery and incense burners. It also sells "functional art" created by a stock of Japanese and international artists, from whimsical picture frames and paper weights to unique soap dishes and bookends. Definitely worth a browse.

The first stoplight north on Aoyama-dori marks Omotesando-dori, which is flanked on both sides by huge stone lanterns. Turn left (west) onto this wide, tree-lined avenue, certainly one of Tokyo's most attractive boulevards. Closed off to vehicular traffic on Sunday afternoons, it becomes a pedestrian's promenade, the perfect place to observe young Japanese dressed to kill as they walk up and down in twos and in groups. On Saturdays and Sundays, young entre-preneurs set up shop along the sidewalk, hawking jewelry, hats, some artwork, and items they've imported from other Asian countries. One of the first buildings to your left will be the:

13. **Hanae Mori Building,** 3-6-1 Kita-Aoyama, designed by Japanese architect Kenzo Tange and housing the entire

collection of Hanae Mori, from casual wear to evening wear. Check out the front-window displays—they're always interesting. On the fifth floor is the upscale L'Orangerie de Paris, while in the basement is the Antique Market, with individual stallkeepers selling Japanese and European china, jewelry, clothing, watches, lacquerware, lamps, and vases, including many art deco objects. Prices are high. It's open from 11am to 7pm; some stalls are closed on Thursday.

Almost next door is:

14. **Shu Uemura,** 5-1-3 Jingumae (tel. 3486-0048), a chain of highly successful cosmetic stores. With open products customers can sample and mix, it features cosmetics, blush, and eyeshadow in incredible rainbow colors and is open daily from 10am to 8pm.

On your right you'll see something that probably wouldn't catch your attention anywhere else but is highly unusual in Tokyo:

15. **Dojunkai Apartments.** They were built in the mid-1920s after the Great Kanto Earthquake, when a growing number of the middle class decided they'd rather live in an apartment in the middle of the city than a long commute away in the suburbs. Several such apartment complexes were built, but this is one of the few that still remain. Each apartment is privately owned, and some have been turned into galleries and shops. With their ivy-covered walls and clumps of shady trees, the apartments look quite cozy and homey. With land prices the way they are, though, the Dojunkai Apartments may well be an endangered species.

To your left you'll pass Genrokusushi (described below under "Take a Break") and then you'll see the orange pillars and Asian facade of Tokyo's best-known souvenir shop, the:

16. **Oriental Bazaar,** 5-9-13 Jingumae (tel. 3400-3933). Although some expatriates in Tokyo may tell you that this store is the Disneyland of souvenir shops, I contend that it's the best place in Tokyo for one-stop souvenir hunting because it offers the largest selections of traditional Japanese products in town. Its three floors of souvenir and gift items include cotton and silk kimono (including great bargains in used kimono), woodblock prints (antique, reproduction, and contemporary), paper products, fans,

Japanese swords, lamps, vases, Imari and Kutani porcelain, sake sets, Japanese dolls, pearls, hibachi, chopsticks, and even some antiques. If you're looking for something inexpensive to buy for office co-workers, neighbors, or friends, I recommend the Japanese paper wallets (good for checkbook covers) located in a corner of the basement. Other good gift buys include cardboard coasters with scenes of famous woodblock prints, chopsticks, fans, and small prints, all of which are inexpensive and easy to pack. This store will also ship purchases home for you. It's open every day except Thursday from 9:30am to 6:30pm.

Just a stone's throw from Oriental Bazaar is:

17. **Vivre 21,** 5-10-1 Jingumae, a sleek, white building filled with fashionable boutiques selling designer clothing by Kenzo, Thierry Mugler, Jean-Paul Gaultier, and others. On the ground floor is a concession of Häagen-Dazs ice cream, while the basement has an interesting shop selling kitchenware and a café. Vivre 21 is open daily from 11am to 8pm.

Just past Shakey's, also on the left side, is:

18. **Kiddy Land,** 6-1-9 Jingumae (tel. 3409-3431), which sells gag gifts and a great deal more than just toys. In addition to the usual games, puzzles, stuffed animals, and kiddy diversions, there's also enough to amuse nondiscerning adults, including temporary tattoos, fake breasts made of rubber, and who knows what else. You could spend an hour here browsing, but the store is often so crowded with teenagers that you may end up rushing for the door. It's open daily from 10am to 8pm, closed the third Tuesday of every month.

Take a Break There are several inexpensive dining and drinking spots along this stretch of Omotesando-dori. **Genrokusushi,** 5-8-5 Jingumae (tel. 3498-3968), is a budget sushi bar that uses a conveyor belt to deliver plates of food, all priced the same, to customers seated at the counter. There's also take-out sushi, in case you want to pack yourself a little something to eat later in Yoyogi Park. It's open daily from 11am to 9pm. Beside Kiddy Land is **Café de Ropé,** 6-1-8 Jingumae (tel. 3406-6845), Harajuku's oldest outdoor café and the perennial hangout of Tokyo's "beautiful people." In the wintertime a plastic tarp and heaters keep the place in operation. It's open daily from 11am to 11pm.

The first big intersection you come to on Omotesando-dori is Meiji-dori. Straight ahead on the left is:

19. **Chicago,** 6-31-21 Jingumae (tel. 3409-5017), which sells second-hand clothing, including jeans, baseball shirts, and '50s, '60s, and '70s clothing. Most interesting for visitors is its used kimono and yukata, most very reasonably priced and located toward the back of the basement store. It's open daily from 11am to 8pm.

On the corner of the Omotesando and Meiji-dori intersection is:

20. **La Forêt,** 1-11-6 Jingumae (tel. 3475-0411), a fashion department store filled with trendy shoe and clothing boutiques. The lower floors tend to be less expensive—they get progressively more expensive with each floor higher up. It's open daily from 11am to 8pm.

Behind La Forêt is one of my favorite museums, the:

21. **Ota Memorial Museum of Art** (Ota Kinen Bijutsukan), 1-10-10 Jingumae (tel. 3403-0880). This great museum features the private ukiyo-e (woodblock print) collection of the late Seizo Ota, who early in life recognized the importance of ukiyo-e as an art form and dedicated his life to its preservation. Among the museum's 12,000 prints are famous works by Japan's top masters, including Harunobu Suzuki, Utamaro Kitagawa, Sharaku Toshusai, Hokusai Katsushika, and Hiroshige Utagawa. Exhibitions are changed monthly, with descriptions of the displays in English. The museum itself is delightful, with such traditional touches as bamboo screens, stone pathways, and even a small tearoom which sells Japanese sweets. As in a Japanese home, take off your shoes at the entryway. It's open Tuesday to Sunday from 10:30am to 5:30pm; closed from the 27th of each month for exhibition changes.

Return to the front entrance of La Forêt, turning left out of La Forêt and heading north on Meiji-dori. To your left will soon be Dear Kid's La Forêt, with expensive clothing for tots, and after a minute's walk you'll see the sign for

The World of Ukiyo-e

Of all forms of Japanese art, none is probably more colorful or insightful than ukiyo-e, or woodblock prints. They are the windows to life in Edo, with scenes of travelers, the roads they traveled, beautiful courtesans, and Kabuki actors. Depicting the social life of Edo's entertainers, merchants, and townspeople from the 17th to the 19th century, ukiyo-e began as a popular art form among the lower classes, dismissed by the well-to-do as being too plebeian and indecent. Only after Westerners discovered ukiyo-e—through examples sent back to Europe, sometimes as wrapping paper—was woodblock printing elevated to a respected art, becoming the rage of the day.

Two of the best-known ukiyo-e artists are Hiroshige and Hokusai, who specialized in landscapes. Hiroshige's most famous work is "Fifty-three Stages of the Tokaido Highway," while Hokusai is remembered for his "Thirty-six Views of Mount Fuji." Other works by Hiroshige are "Noted Places of Edo" and "One Hundred Scenic Spots of Edo." Sharaku is famous for his Kabuki portraits; Utamaro, Harunobu, and Kiyonaga specialized in portraits of beautiful women.

During the Edo Period, ukiyo-e required the cooperative efforts of three different artists—the painter, an engraver, and a printer. First the artist drew his picture in black and white on translucent paper, which was pasted face down on a block of cherry wood. The engraver then sawed and scraped until every detail of the print came into view, completing his work by using a knife and then chisels to reproduce the picture on the block. Color was applied with a brush, the impression having been made by hand with the assistance of a pad. Gradations of tone and color were often obtained from a single block; different colors usually called for more blocks, one for each color used. Much artistic feeling went into the printing of ukiyo-e, so that printers were often just as valued as the painters.

Takeshita Guchi on a stoplight. We'll come back to this tiny pedestrian lane, but if it's the first or fourth Sunday of the month you might want to continue walking north a few minutes until on your left you see:

22. **Togo Shrine.** It's dedicated to Admiral Heihachiro Togo, who was in charge of the fleet that defeated the Russian navy in 1905 in the Russo-Japanese War. Nowadays, the shrine is most popular for its flea market, when everything from old chests, dolls, and inkwells to kitchen utensils, lacquerware, and pottery are for sale, spread out on cloths on a sidewalk that meanders under trees to the shrine. The market is especially good for bargains in used kimono. Beginning early in the morning, it usually goes on until about 3:30pm.

   Retrace your steps back in the direction of La Forêt. Across the street on your right you'll see a wide set of steps, often filled with people taking a breather. They lead to:

23. **Designers Collezione,** 4-32-16 Meiji-dori (tel. 3479-2457), a chain of discount name-brand outlets offering imported clothing. Open daily from noon to 8pm, it carries clothing by Armani, Versace, and other designers, with selections changing with the seasons.

   To your right is:

24. **Takeshita-dori,** a pedestrian-only street that is best recognized by its shoulder-to-shoulder crowd on Sunday afternoons. Lined nonstop with stores, it's often jam-packed with young people—usually Japanese teenagers—who come in from the countryside to hunt for bargains in inexpensive clothing, shoes, music, sunglasses, jewelry, and more. It's all there, if only you can find it through the hordes.

   After inching your way along this narrow lane with the flow of humanity, turn left at the top end of Takeshita-dori, where you'll see:

25. **Harajuku Station.** It's one of Tokyo's most picturesque and oldest stations, built in 1924 to reflect the local flavor of the neighborhood. Soon, across from the station on your left, you'll see a small enclosed area called:

26. **Green Hill Park,** where young vendors set up stalls of clothing and accessories. You can find bargains here, though

some of the leather-studded items may be too bizarre for the folks back home.

Just past the station, turn right and walk over the bridge above the tracks to the entrance of:

27. **Meiji Jingu Shrine,** which in its peacefulness is a huge contrast to the action of Harajuku. This is Tokyo's most venerable shrine, opened in 1920 in dedication to Emperor and Empress Meiji, who were instrumental in opening Japan to the rest of the world a hundred years ago. Becoming the 122nd emperor in 1868 while still a teenager, Emperor Meiji oversaw Japan's transition from a feudal state to a modern capitalist nation. Two large torii, built of cypress more than 1,700 years old and Japan's largest torii made of wood, give dramatic entrance to the shrine's grounds, once the estate of a daimyo lord. The shaded pathway is lined with trees, shrubs, and a dense woods, with most of the trees and shrubs donated by people from all over Japan and therefore a good representation of flora from throughout the country. On the way to the shrine you can stop off at the Iris Garden (admission charged), spectacular for its more than 100 varieties of irises in bloom in late June and July. A stream meanders through the Iris Garden, and if you follow it to its source, you'll find a famous spring, discovered more than 400 years ago by a famous feudal lord and still drinkable. The shrine itself is a fine example of dignified and restrained Shinto architecture, made of Japanese cypress topped with green copper roofs. Within a 10-minute walk north of the shrine complex is the Treasure Museum, which charges admission and contains personal effects of Emperor Meiji and Empress Shoken, including garments, books, furniture, and photographs. Incidentally, Meiji Shrine is the most popular place to be on New Year's Day, when two million people crowd onto its grounds to welcome in the new year. The shrine grounds are open daily from 5am to 6:30pm; the Treasure Museum is open from 9am to 5pm (4:30pm in winter), closed the third Friday of every month.

Retrace your steps back to the entrance of the shrine, turn right, and you'll see a wide boulevard that, if it's Sunday, has been closed to traffic and is filled with a mass of people. Here, from about noon to 5pm, are the:

28. **Harajuku performers.** In what is Tokyo's best free show, everyone from rock 'n' rollers to musicians converges to do his or her thing, surrounded by crowds of onlookers eager for a show. It all started in the 1970s when a group of kids got together and began dancing to music they brought with them on their portable cassette players. The number of young performers grew, until by the mid-1980s there were as many as several hundred teenagers dancing in the street, dressed either in colorful circuslike clothing or styles of the 1950s, with crinoline skirts, black leather jackets, fluffy sweaters, and slicked back hair. As far as Japanese society was concerned, these kids were dropouts. After all, how dare they dress up in outrageous costumes, and, even worse, make public spectacles of themselves by dancing unabashedly in the middle of the street in Tokyo's fashionable Harajuku district? However, despite the opinion among older Japanese that these kids are somehow counterculture, they are actually quite conventional. They don't drink alcohol, and most bring their outrageous clothing with them, changing in the public restroom. And similar to most undertakings in Japan, there is group mentality even here. Each group has its own cassette player, music, leader, costumes, and dance routines. Individual dancing is out, and if by chance you simply joined in, the other dancers would regard you with astonishment and consider you rather weird. The fun consists in simply wandering about, observing group after group. In recent years, rock bands have replaced most of the dancers, set up side by side along the street and playing a cacophony of styles. I wouldn't be surprised to learn that for most of the musicians, this is the only chance they get to play. In this carnival-like atmosphere there are also stalls selling everything from fried noodles to roasted corn on the cob to a kind of Japanese omelet.

    That building beside the street performers is the:

29. **National Gymnasium,** designed by Kenzo Tange as the indoor sports arena of the 1964 Olympics. Opposite the sports complex is:

30. **Yoyogi Park,** a huge expanse of green popular with families, couples, and students. Once used by the Japanese army as a drilling ground and then, after World War II, by U.S.

Occupation forces as a barracks, it was the site of the athletes' village for the 1964 Olympics. It contains a wild bird sanctuary, as well as playgrounds and a cycling course for children. Park space in Tokyo is woefully inadequate—just 4.52 square meters per capita, compared to 45.7 per person in Washington, D.C. The park is open every day except Monday, from 5am to 8pm (5pm in winter).

The closest station is Harajuku on the Yamanote Line.

Take a Break After you've observed the Sunday dancers of Harajuku, paid your respects at Meiji Jingu Shrine, and fought your way through the crowds, you're probably ready to imbibe a drink or two. One of the closest bars to Harajuku Station is **Stage Y2,** 1-13-12 Jingumae (tel. 3478-1031), located to the left as you walk on Omotesando-dori away from the station in the direction of Meiji-dori. Open daily from 10am to 11:30pm, this sleek and modern black building offers some outdoor sidewalk tables, as well as airy indoor seating in a room reminiscent of a greenhouse, minus the plants. In addition to coffee, beer, soft drinks, and cocktails, it offers an assortment of dishes and snacks, including pasta, pizza, soups, and sandwiches, most reasonably priced. For another indoor bar in the area, take the small side street that runs beside Café de Ropé (mentioned earlier in this walk) to **Oh God,** 6-7-18 Jingumae (tel. 3406-3206). It shows free foreign films every night beginning at about 6pm, ranging from James Bond thrillers and the films of the late German director Werner Fassbinder to B-grade horror flicks. Mellow and dimly lit, it's open daily from 6pm to 6am. My favorite place for a meal in Harajuku is **Beer Market Doma,** in the basement of the Ga-Z Building, 6-5-3 Jingumae (tel. 3498-7251), just off the intersection of Omotesando-dori and Meiji-dori. Offering an exotic mix of Chinese, Japanese, Thai, and other Asian cuisine at very reasonable prices, it has both a cafeteria with a dozen or so dishes, as well as a table-service menu. Lunch is served daily from 11:30am to 2pm, while dinner is served daily from 5 to 11:30pm.

SHINJUKU–NEW TOWN

Start: Shinjuku Gyoen National Garden. Station: Shinjuku-Gyoen-mae on the Marunouchi Line, then exit 1 for Shinjuku Gyoen.

Finish: Hanazono Jinja Shrine, Yasukun-dori. Station: Shinjuku San-chome.

Time: Allow approximately five hours, not including Take a Break.

Best Times: Weekdays, when attractions aren't as crowded; or, if you like crowds, on Sunday, when Shinjuku-dori becomes a pedestrian promenade. If the nightlife in Kabuki-cho is your main interest, on Friday or Saturday, when the district is in full swing.

Worst Times: On Monday, when Shinjuku-Gyoen and the observatory in the Tokyo Metropolitan Government building are closed.

To describe a place as "a study in contrasts" is an overworked cliché, and yet Shinjuku is exactly that. It's the home of Tokyo's new city hall, along with towering office buildings, first-class hotels, and department stores. But Shinjuku is also home to Tokyo's raunchiest nightlife district, with love hotels, peep shows, massage parlors, and strip joints. Upon closer reflection, maybe this coupling of politics and business with nighttime diversions isn't such a strange match after all, especially in Japan where hostesses and prostitutes have replaced geisha and courtesans as mothers to the male ego, arranged marriages still take place, and where fidelity has never been a moral issue. In any case, tending to the needs of men has been Shinjuku's role from the very start.

Located on the western edge of the Yamanote Line loop, Shinjuku originated as a post station in 1698, to serve the needs of feudal lords and their retainers making the biennial trek to and from their fiefdoms. Shinjuku's name, in fact, means "new lodgings," and situated an easy day's walk from Nihombashi, it made a convenient first-night stopover. It wasn't long, however, before it became apparent that Shinjuku's lodgings were nothing more than thinly disguised brothels (which probably encouraged more than a few travelers to get an early day's start), and they were soon closed by the Tokugawa shogunate in a crackdown against unlicensed pleasure quarters. Logistics eventually won, however, and Shinjuku reopened as a post town in 1772. By 1790 there were more than 50 inns—or brothels—in operation.

For more than a century Shinjuku remained an isolated outpost, far from the main business districts of Hibiya and Nihombashi. Then, in 1923, the Great Kanto Earthquake struck, laying to waste buildings in central Tokyo. Shinjuku was hardly touched by the disaster, prompting many businesses to relocate there in their haste to maintain operations. In 1971, Shinjuku's first skyscraper was erected with the opening of the Keio Plaza Hotel, setting a dramatic precedent for things to come. Today more than a dozen skyscrapers dot the Shinjuku skyline, far more than anywhere else in Japan. With the opening of Tokyo's new city hall in 1991, Shinjuku's transformation into the capital's upstart business district was complete.

Shinjuku is divided by Shinjuku Station, the nation's busiest, into an east and west side. The western part is its respectable —and rather stodgy—face, boasting the nation's greatest concentration of skyscrapers with its thousands of office workers and a number of hotels. Eastern Shinjuku is known for its shopping and nightlife, especially Kabuki-cho, a thriving amusement and entertainment district. There are few cultural attractions in Shinjuku (though all of Kabuki-cho might arguably offer more cultural insight than any museum could). Since Shinjuku's east and west sides are as different—literally—as night and day, you may wish to shorten the following tour to suit your interests. If you want to complete the entire tour, start out after lunch or in the early afternoon so that you don't arrive in Kabuki-cho too early.

● ● ● ● ● ● ● ● ● ● ● ● ● ● ●

After exiting from Shinjuku-Gyoen-mae station, make your way to the Shinjuku entrance of:

1. **Shinjuku Gyoen National Garden** (tel. 3350-0151), formerly the private estate of a feudal lord and then of the imperial family. Opened to the public after World War II, it's considered one of the most important gardens of the Meiji era and is one of the city's largest city parks. Because of its convenient location in the center of the city, it's a popular destination for school groups and families on warm days, with wide grassy expanses inviting picnics and playing. Its 144 acres also contain three distinctly different styles of gardens, making it a wonderful park for a stroll. The French formal garden, planted at the turn of the century with an avenue of plane trees bordering a rose bed, is probably Shinjuku Gyoen's most impressive section, though the Japanese traditional garden is the most picturesque, especially during the blooming of wisteria or azaleas. The Taiwan Kaku Pavilion in the Japanese garden was built in 1927, in commemoration of Emperor Hirohito's wedding, and resembles an upper-class Taiwanese mansion with its curved roof and eight-sided windows. When Hirohito died in 1989, his funeral was held here in Shinjuku Gyoen, with representatives from more than 160 countries in attendance. There's also an English countryside landscape garden, and a variety of flowering trees and shrubs ranging from the garden's 1,500 cherry trees to hydrangeas, chrysanthemums, tulip trees, cedars, and cypresses. The greenhouse contains more than 1,700 tropical and subtropical plant species, including more than 300 orchids. Shinjuku Gyoen is open Tuesday through Sunday from 9am to 4:30pm (you must enter by 4pm) and admission is charged.

 Take a Break Inside Shinjuku Gyoen, near the park's Shinjuku (north) gate, is the **Shinjuku Park**

Restaurant which offers a wide mix of Japanese and Western generic dishes, including spaghetti, shrimp pilaf, shrimp gratin, udon, soba, and set meals, at reasonable prices. Just outside the park's Shinjuku gate is **La Primavera,** 2-5-15 Shinjuku (tel. 3354-7873), which serves great Italian food at reasonable prices, including a good set lunch. It's open Monday to Saturday from 11:30am to 2pm and 6 to 10pm.

Exit Shinjuku Gyoen via the same gate you entered the park (Shinjuku gate), and then walk straight ahead two short blocks to where the lane ends at a busy thoroughfare, Shinjuku-dori, where you should turn left and walk west. After a five-minute walk you will soon see:

2. **Isetan,** 3-14-1 Shinjuku (tel. 3352-1111). This department store, a favorite among foreigners living in Tokyo, has a good selection of conservative clothing appropriate for work, as well as contemporary and fashionable styles, including designer clothes. In addition to boutiques carrying the creations of such well-known fashion moguls and design houses as Issey Miyake, Kansai, Yohji Yamamoto, Hanae Mori, Gucci, Fendi, Chanel, Sonia Rykiel, Donna Karan, Jean-Paul Gaultier, and Rei Kawakubo, it also boasts a New Creator's Space on the ground floor, unique among Japanese department stores which are generally reluctant to carry anything but the tried and true. It features up and coming Japanese designers, including works by Masahiro Miyazaki, Osamu Maeda, Yoshiki Hishinuma, and Yuji Hamada. Isetan also has a great kimono department, along with all the accessories that go with the national traditional dress (shoes, purses, obi), a well-known art gallery on the eighth floor of its annex, an arts and crafts section with changing exhibits, and a promotional hall on the fifth floor that serves as the store's outlet for seasonal bargains (Isetan's summer and winter designer sales are among the city's best—I've picked up some great bargains here). Isetan is open every day except Wednesday from 10am to 7pm.
   Across the street is:

3. **Marui Fashion,** 3-30-16 Shinjuku (tel. 3354-0101), the main shop of five Marui department stores in Shinjuku, each with different merchandise. Aimed at young consumers, Marui offers easy-to-obtain credit cards, making it a

Shinjuku—New Town

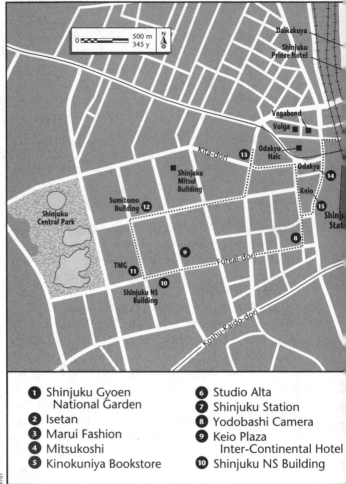

Map legend:

1. Shinjuku Gyoen National Garden
2. Isetan
3. Marui Fashion
4. Mitsukoshi
5. Kinokuniya Bookstore
6. Studio Alta
7. Shinjuku Station
8. Yodobashi Camera
9. Keio Plaza Inter-Continental Hotel
10. Shinjuku NS Building

natural for young shoppers who are buying clothes or setting up households for the first time. Marui Fashion carries both men's and women's clothing; in its basement is Virgin Megastore, with more than 100,000 CD titles ranging from rock and jazz to classical and Japanese. Other Marui stores in the immediate neighborhood include Marui Interior with its household goods, Marui Men's, and Young-kan with more youthful fashion. All Marui stores are open from 11am to 8pm; closed some Wednesdays. Department stores used to be closed religiously one day a week, but now there doesn't seem to be any rhyme or reason as to why a store may be

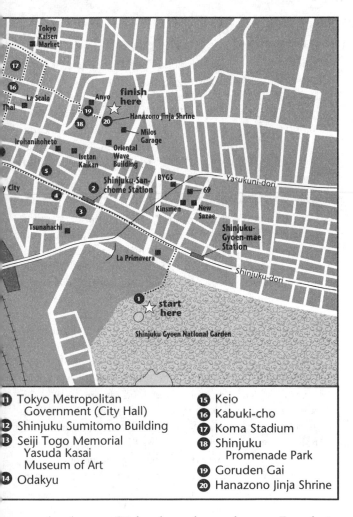

closed on one Wednesday and open the next. Even the information-booth staff was flustered when I asked—some department stores simply pass out pocket calendars with the closed days marked

Just past Marui Fashion, to the west on Shinjuku-dori, is another department store:

4. **Mitsukoshi,** 3-29-1 Shinjuku (tel. 3354-1111), the Shinjuku branch of one of Japan's oldest department stores. It's open from 10am to 7pm, closed some Mondays.

Across the street is:

5. **Kinokuniya Bookstore,** 3-17-7 Shinjuku (tel. 3354-0131), one of Tokyo's largest bookstores. (It's also one of Shinjuku's oldest establishments, first opened in 1927 and selling not books but charcoal; in fact this part of Shinjuku used to be Tokyo's main wholesale area for charcoal.) Look for English titles on the sixth floor, which carries more than 50,000 foreign books and magazines, including books on Japan and dictionaries and textbooks for those studying Japanese. It's open daily from 10am to 8pm; closed the third Wednesday of every month.

☕ **Take a Break**   **Tsunahachi（つな八）,** 3-31-8 Shinjuku (tel. 3352-1012), is a tempura restaurant founded in 1923 and now boasting more than 40 branch restaurants in Japan. This is its main shop, located on the small side street that runs between Marui Fashion and Mitsukoshi—look for a small, unassuming two-story building, the most traditional one on the street. Open daily from 11am to 10:30pm, it offers reasonably priced set meals (called teishoku) for lunch. Department stores almost always have one floor devoted to restaurants, usually on one of the top floors. Since most have plastic-food displays, ordering is easy. On the seventh floor of **Isetan** are more than a dozen outlets, offering Japanese food ranging from sushi and tempura to tonkatsu (breaded pork) and eel, as well as international cuisine such as Chinese, Italian, French, and Indian. Restaurants are open from 11am to 10pm, closed some Wednesdays. **Mitsukoshi** has a few restaurants on its eighth floor, open every day, except some Mondays, from 11am to 8pm and offering sushi, soba, Chinese dishes, and snacks.

At the west end of Shinjuku-dori is a large outdoor screen, belonging to:

6. **Studio Alta.** Since Japanese are more likely to socialize in public places rather than entertain at home, almost every neighborhood in central Tokyo has a well-known meeting spot. This is Shinjuku's, below the big screen.

Ahead of you is:

7. **Shinjuku Station,** Japan's largest station and a formidable one to navigate. When it first opened back in 1885, it served

only freight, primarily coal and textiles. In 1906 it began passenger service, and by 1928 it was already the busiest station in the nation. Today more than two million passengers pass through Shinjuku Station daily. If you want to see Tokyo at its craziest, go to Shinjuku Station at 8:30am (preferably by taxi), when you have no choice but to go with the flow and when commuters are packed so tightly into trains that no one can move an inch. A friend of mine told me she's been in such a packed compartment that her feet were lifted off the floor; another time she feared her arm would break when a sea of people swept her briefcase along with them. There are more than 60 exits from Shinjuku Station, a maze made even more confusing by an underground shopping arcade called "My City" with more than 250 outlets. I get lost almost every time I enter Shinjuku Station, although navigation is much easier than it used to be—just a decade ago, there weren't even any signs in English.

You can avoid Shinjuku Station altogether by turning left before the station, walking past it to Koshu-Kaido-dori and turning right, and then right again after the Lumine department store. Otherwise, if you're up to the challenge, take the Marunouchi subway entrance below the Studio Alta screen and head west on the Metro Promenade, an underground passage that stretches all the way to Shinjuku San-chome and the west entrance to the Marunouchi line. Keep walking straight, past the Marunouchi Line entrance, following signs that say "West Exit" and then "Exit 15." When you reach the busy underground square, walk diagonally across it, past the large fountains and a counter of the Information Bureau of Tokyo (stop here for directions if you want), turning left and then walking up the stairs of Exit 8. If you've made it, give yourself a deserved pat on the back. By the way, you probably noticed that Shinjuku Station is one of Tokyo's domains of the homeless. Could be they entered the station looking like everyone else, headed home after work and a few rounds of beer, but got hopelessly lost and never found their way out again.

Straight ahead is a neon sign that says "Head Store," the main shop of:

8. **Yodobashi Camera,** 1-11-1 Nishi-Shinjuku (tel. 3346-1010), one of the largest camera shops in the world. It has

more than 30,000 items in stock, including display cameras you can pick up and inspect, film (at prices about as good as you'll find anywhere in Tokyo), watches, calculators, typewriters, and cassette players. Its tax-free section is on the second floor and even though prices are marked, you can still bargain. Hours here are from 9:30am to 8:30pm daily.

From Yodobashi head straight west toward the futuristic-looking skyscraper, passing more discount shops. There are a number of camera shops here, making this part of Shinjuku a good place to comparison-shop. You'll also see maps posted of West Shinjuku, a welcome recent addition. Cross the street with the stoplight and continue west—you are now on Fureai-dori. On your right you'll see:

9. **Keio Plaza Inter-Continental Hotel,** built in 1971 as Shinjuku's first skyscraper. At 47 stories, it's still Tokyo's tallest hotel, and its brilliant white exterior is composed of pre-cast concrete panels, the first application of this technique in Japan. It used to offer unparalleled views of Mt. Fuji—but Shinjuku's new city hall put an end to that.

Continuing west, to your left you'll see the:

10. **Shinjuku NS Building,** noted for its see-though outdoor elevator. Built in 1982, it also has a spectacular atrium that stretches all the way to the top of the building—30 floors high and capped with a glass roof consisting of 6,000 sheets of glass. In a country where space is at a premium, this flaunting of space is a statement of luxury. The ground floor lobby boasts a giant Seiko clock. Restaurants—some with great views—are on the 29th and 30th floor. If heights don't bother you, try walking across the bridge that stretches across the atrium on the 29th floor.

Take a Break Among the NS Building's restaurants, on the 29th floor there's **The Spaghetti Factory** offering inexpensive platters of pasta and **Suehiro** with its steaks, shabu-shabu, and sukiyaki. On the 30th floor are **The Wine Bar** and almost a dozen other outlets offering Japanese and Western food. If you're most interested in the view, choose a restaurant facing west or south. Restaurants here are open daily from about 11:30am to 9:30pm. Other buildings with restaurants or cafés on high floors offering a view include the **Tokyo Metropolitan Government** office, which has a self-service snack bar in its 45th-floor observatory, and the **Sumitomo Building,** which has more than 22 outlets on its top four floors offering everything from Kobe beef and Chinese cuisine to salads and snacks, most open daily from about 11am to 9:30pm.

That futuristic-looking building you've been walking toward, with the Gothic-style towers made of granite and glass and the latticed windows, is the:

11. **Tokyo Metropolitan Government (TMG) office,** 2-8-1 Nishi-Shinjuku (tel. 5321-1111), designed by one of Japan's most well-known architects, Kenzo Tange, and completed in 1991 as Tokyo's new city hall. Actually there are three buildings that comprise the complex—TMG No. 1, TMG No. 2, and the Metropolitan Assembly Building. TMG No. 1, the one to the right (north), is the most important one for visitors, for it offers one of the best views of Tokyo—absolutely free. Rising 48 stories above ground and at 656 feet the tallest building in Shinjuku, it boasts two observatories, located on the 45th floors of both the North and South Towers, with access from the first floor. Be sure to pick up an English guide to the TMG and its observatories from the information desks on either the first or second floors. Both observatories offer the same the great view and have a self-serve snack bar in the middle, where you can relax over a cup of coffee, ice cream, or cheesecake. On clear days you can see Mt. Fuji. To the west down below you can see Shinjuku Central Park with its wooded areas, jogging paths, large man-made waterfall, and children's playground.

You are requested to get off at the second floor when descending, where you'll find exhibitions relating to local government and its history in prewar and postwar times. Although explanations are in Japanese only, the videos and photos are self-explanatory, providing interesting glimpses into the city's past.

Exit TMG No. 1 from the north door. Straight ahead to the north is the Century Hyatt Hotel; north of that is the Tokyo Hilton International. Across from the Century Hyatt (catty-corner from TMG No. 1) is a white triangular building, the:

12. **Shinjuku Sumitomo Building,** 2-6-1 Nishi-Shinjuku, with an entrance on its east side. Nicknamed the Sankaku (Triangular) Building, it's hollow inside—in the middle of the first-floor lobby is a triangular prism from where you can look upwards to the top of the building. On the 51st floor is a small observation room with free admittance; it used to offer the best view of Shinjuku before the opening of city hall. Not as high as city hall's observatory, it nonetheless offers the best vantage for seeing and photographing the TMG complex. Restaurants with great views of the city are located on the top four floors.

Take the first-floor exit from the Sumitomo Building, the one in front of the escalator, and walk straight ahead through the ivy-covered brick archway. To your left will be a multi-level bicycle parking garage—a necessity in such a crowded city. Upon emerging into the open air, down below to your left you'll see a brick plaza, complete with fountain and trees, which is skyscraper city's most pleasant place to hang out during nice weather. You might want to stop for a breather here—and if you must, there's a fast-food hamburger joint here too.

Just past the square, take a left into the Mitsui Building next door and take the escalator up one floor, turning right to exit the building and then turning left. Ahead is a skyscraper with slanting walls, the Yasuda Kasai Building, our next destination. To reach it, cross the street at the stoplight and then turn right. Is it windy enough for you? Everytime I come here I'm lashed by winds howling through skyscraper canyons. Inside the Yasuda Kasai Building, on the 42nd floor, is the:

13. **Seiji Togo Memorial Yasuda Kasai Museum of Art,** 1-26-1 Nishi-Shinjuku (tel. 3349-3081). It contains the works of Seiji Togo, known for his portraits of young girls, but the most remarkable aspect of the museum is that it's home to Van Gogh's *Sunflowers,* bought in 1987 for a record $40 million dollars at the height of Japan's optimistic bubble economy. There are also two Renoirs, a Gauguin, a Cézanne, a Rodin, and a view of Shinjuku. It's a rather somber place

for those sunny sunflowers—the building itself houses an insurance company, with a no-nonsense atmosphere that precludes observatories, shops, and even restaurants. The museum, which charges admission, is open every day except Monday from 9:30am to 5pm (enter by 4:30pm).

Turn left out of the Yasuda Kasai Building and head east on Kita-dori, crossing the street at the street light and continuing east to Shinjuku Station. If you're interested in more shopping, above Shinjuku Station on the west side are:

14. **Odakyu department store** and its annex **Odakyu Halc,** 1-1-3 Nishi-Shinjuku (tel. 3342-1111), open every day except Tuesday from 10am to 7pm, and:

15. **Keio department store,** 1-1-4 Nishi-Shinjuku (tel. 3342-2111), open from 10am to 7pm every day except Thursday. Both stores are popular with commuters, who stop off for everyday products or to pick up something for dinner from the food departments. In front of Keio are a handful of independent workers once plentiful throughout the city but now a dying breed—shoe polishers. Stop here to sit and relax at one of the makeshift stations and to have your shoes polished or repaired. Most of the workers are elderly; few young Japanese today are willing to follow in their footsteps.

Take a Break   If the weather is fine, one of the best places to stop off for a beer and a snack is on top of a building—favored spots in Japan for beer gardens. There's one atop **Keio** department store, open from the end of April to the end of September daily, from 5 to 9:30pm. A plastic display case shows what's available, including mugs of foaming beer. Buy tickets for food and drink at the ticket window, and bemoan the fact that beer gardens across the country try imitating nature with plastic grass and fake flowers or plants. It's one of the incongruities of Japan—how a people who give so much attention to the beauty of flower arranging, the aesthetics of the tea ceremony, and even the wrapping of a package think nothing of adorning their environment with gaudy plastic flora.

Although most of the night action in Shinjuku takes place east of the station, the west side also has a small area of inexpensive restaurants and bars. Two of my favorite are located on the second alley behind Odakyu Halc. **Vagabond,** 1-4-20 Nishi-Shinjuku (tel. 3348-9109), is a cozy jazz piano bar, open Monday to Saturday from 5:30 to 11:30pm and on Sunday from 4:30 to 10:30pm. There's no cover charge per se, though there is an obligatory snack charge for the chips or snack brought automatically to your table. This second-floor establishment is owned by the effervescent Mr. Matsuoka, who loves having foreign guests and speaks perfect English. Down the street, on the corner, is **Volga (ボルガ),** 1-4 Nishi-Shinjuku (tel. 3342-4996), a yakitori-ya with an open grill facing the street and an ivy-covered two-story brick facade. With its smoky, simply decorated interior (plastic plants!) and wooden chairs and tables, it looks like a place time forgot and has a slightly bohemian atmosphere. It's open Monday through Saturday from 5:30 to 10:30pm.

If you've had enough for the day and don't feel up to Shinjuku's nightlife, disappear into the labyrinth of Shinjuku to search for the commuter train or subway that will take you to your next destination. Good luck.

Otherwise, walk north on the road that runs between Odakyu Halc and the station, cross the busy street, turn right and walk under the overhead tracks in the direction of Shinjuku Prince Hotel. You are now on Yasukuni-dori, one of Shinjuku's main thoroughfares. Walk east on Yasukuni-dori, past the Prince Hotel, McDonald's, and the bank building on the left, turning left at the lighted archway that leads into a pedestrian zone of neon signs. You are now in the heart of:

16. **Kabuki-cho,** famous all over Japan as Shinjuku's entertainment and amusement district. Its name stems from a plan adopted after World War II to build a Kabuki theater here. The plan never materialized but the name stuck, and instead of a Kabuki theater Shinjuku got one of Japan's first strip shows. Today Kabuki-cho covers several square blocks, chock full with peep shows, strip shows, pornography shops, massage parlors, love hotels (where rooms rent by the hour), turkish baths, and panty-less coffee shops. Although prostitution was banned in Japan upon insistence of U.S.

Occupation forces after World War II, authorities tend to look the other way. There are also plenty of legitimate establishments here, primarily restaurants and bars, so that Kabuki-cho draws a strange mix of clientele, from businessmen who weave about in happy drunkenness to couples out on a date. Even high school students like Shinjuku for its many video-game parlors. There are also plenty of out-of-towners, eager for a look at their capital's most infamous center of sin. This being Japan, the streets of Kabuki-cho are all pretty tame and harmless, so I had no qualms about taking my mother for a spin here when she came to Tokyo for a visit. If you're a woman traveling alone, however, you may wish to forgo the Kabuki-cho experience. Those drunken businessmen, shorn of their usual reserve, may annoy you with their advances, though they are also easily rebuffed. Alcoholism is not looked upon as a disease in Japan, or even undesirable. Going out with co-workers after hours is encouraged by most companies as a form of bonding; drinking too much is an accepted form of release in an otherwise regimented society. Employees are forgiven for speaking their mind. Underlings get together to complain and let off steam. In the publishing company where I worked, employees thought nothing of coming into work moaning about a hangover. In fact, they were often treated with deference by fellow employees, even when they fell asleep at their desk.

Take a Break There are many inexpensive eating and drinking establishments in Shinjuku. One of these is **Daikokuya (大黒家)**, on the fourth floor of the Naka-Dai Building at 1-27-5 Kabuki-cho (tel. 3202-7272), located in the second block west of Koma Stadium. It's a haven for gluttons, especially those who can put away mountains of food in a short amount of time, since the deal here is all you can eat of shabu-shabu or sukiyaki during a two-hour time limit. For an added sum it's all the beer you can drink as well. Popular with students for its low prices, it's strangely decorated with pseudo cave walls, perhaps harking back to more barbaric times when people chowed down unrestrainedly. It's open Monday to Friday from 5 to 11pm and Saturday and Sunday from 3 to 11pm. For more sophisticated dining, try **Ban-Thai,** 1-23-14 Kabuki-cho (tel. 3207-0068), one of Tokyo's best Thai restaurants and a bit pricey. It's located on the pedestrian street with the neon archway, about halfway between Yasukuni-dori and Koma Stadium, up on the third floor. It's open Monday to Friday from noon to 1am and Saturday and Sunday from 11am to 1am. **Tokyo Kaisen Market,** 2-36-1 Kabuki-cho (tel. 5273-8301), is a great place for fresh seafood. Choose something swimming in its ground-floor tanks, then head upstairs to dine on your catch prepared the way you ordered it. There's also an English menu of dim sum, Chinese side dishes, sashimi, and seafood. It's open Monday to Friday from 5pm to midnight and Saturday and Sunday from noon to midnight. If all you want is a drink in a convivial student pub, head for **Irohanihoheto (いろはにほへと),** 3-15-15 Shinjuku (tel. 3359-1682), on Yasukuni-Dori on the sixth floor of a building next to Isetan Kaikan. Open Sunday through Thursday from 5pm to 11:30pm and on Friday and Saturday from 5pm to 4am, it also offers great snacks and dishes at cheap prices. And finally, for a cup of coffee in an offbeat but refined setting, head for **La Scala,** 1-14-1 Kabuki-cho (tel. 3208-5394), an ivy-covered castle-like coffee shop which looks totally out of place in the madness of Kabuki-cho. Opened in 1954, it offers cups of coffee to the soothing strains of classical music, a restful haven with velvet upholstered chairs, chandeliers, and stained-glass windows. It's open daily from 10am to 11pm.

Assuming you're still on the same pedestrian street as when you entered Kabuki-cho, walk straight north, past flashing neon signs, hawkers touting sex shows, and the crowds. Soon you'll come to:

17. **Koma Stadium,** located in the heart of Kabuki-cho and well known for its theater used for Japan's leading performers, plays, and drama.

Pass Koma Stadium and then turn right. You will soon see Tokyo Kaisen Market to your left, a large wharf-like eating establishment featuring live tanks of seafood (see "Take a Break," above). After a few blocks, turn right at sany street and follow it back to Yasukuni-dori, where you should turn left and head east. To your right you'll pass

Irohanihoheto, an inexpensive pub (described under "Take a Break," above) and Isetan Kaikan. You will then see a sign for Ad Hoc on your right and movie theaters. Here, directly across the street to your left, is a lighted pathway lined with trees, the:

18. **Shinjuku Promenade Park,** with a sign that reads Shinjuku Bunka Center. This is one of Shinjuku's few attempts to create an urban oasis and features gingko trees and small pines. Turn right after the Seiko clock, which brings you to one of Tokyo's oddest places:

19. **Goruden Gai** ("Golden Guy"). It's a miniature neighborhood of a few tiny alleyways leading past even tinier bars, each consisting of just a counter and a few stools. Usually closed to outsiders, these bars cater to regular customers, some of them writers and media personalities. On hot summer evenings, the "mama-san" of these bars sit outside and fan themselves, bathed in soft red lights coming through the open doorways. These aren't brothels, they are simply bars, and the mama-san—well, she's as likely to be a he as a she. With space as valuable as it is, development keeps rearing its ugly head, threatening Goruden Gai with extinction, but for now enjoy the atmosphere of this strange place by walking up and down its few short alleys.

> ☕ **Take a Break** **Anyo (あんよ),** located on the northern-most lane of Goruden Gai, is typical of the dozens of small bars in this quirky neighborhood but is atypical in that it welcomes foreigners. It's owned by a very friendly woman named Ayumi Mori and her husband, Nariyaki, both of whom speak English and have managed the place for more than a quarter of a century. This place is a true find for the opportunity it affords of a different view of Japanese life, but be aware that there's an obligatory table charge and snack charge and that prices can add up. It's open Monday through Saturday from 7pm to 2am.

To the east of Goruden Gai is a small police station with a red light; across the street from the station are steps leading to:

20. **Hanazono Jinja Shrine,** brightly painted in orange and already established before Tokugawa set up his shogunate

in Edo. The shrine is said to promote commercial success, as well as improve soil conditions, making it a convenient place for busy merchants during the days when wealth was measured in rice. The shrine is best known today for a flea market held here on the second and third Sunday of each month from 7am to about 3 or 4pm, which probably provides a certain amount of commercial success to at least some of the vendors.

With your back to the front of the shrine, take a right through the orange torii. About halfway down, to your left, is Milos Garage, a bare basement establishment open from 8pm to 5am daily and catering to young Japanese sporting an Asian version of grunge. Otherwise, the small lane brings you back to Yasukuni-dori. Turn left for the nearest subway station, Shinjuku San-chome.

Take a Break If you turn right at Yasukuni-dori upon exiting from Hanazono Shrine, you will soon come to the **Oriental Wave Building** on your right, at 5-17-13 Shinjuku (tel. 3203-2878). On the ground floor is a chic and breezy café, open daily from 11am to 10pm. On the second floor is Rajini, which offers "Oriental crossover" food in a colonial atmosphere reminiscent of Britain's former Asian strongholds. It's open daily from 5pm to midnight. If you're ready for some partying until dawn, try **Milos Garage,** described above, or head east on Yasukuni-dori, aiming for the BYGS building. The small side street that runs beside BYGS will take you to Shinjuku 2-chome (pronounced "ni-chome"), Shinjuku's gay district. It's here that I was once taken to a host bar featuring young men in crotchless pants. Strangely enough, the clientele included both gay men and groups of giggling young women. The place has since closed down, but Shinjuku is riddled with places bordering on the absurd. It's no longer a gay bar, but one of the district's old-timers is **69,** located behind BYGS in a basement at 2-18-5 Shinjuku (tel. 3341-6358). Playing primarily reggae music, this dive is tiny, and often so packed it reminds me of the Yamanote Line during rush hour. It's popular with young foreigners and Japanese, most of them dancing the night away—at least until midnight, when it closes. In the next building, up on the second floor, is

Kinsmen (tel. 3354-4949), a very civilized gay bar that welcomes customers of both persuasions and with music low enough to encourage conversation. It's open every day except Tuesday from 9pm to 5am. Around the corner is **New Sazae** (tel. 3354-1745), a dive of a place, rowdy and not for the weak-hearted. Customers, who migrate here after other bars in the area have closed down for the night, are a weird mix, and if you get this far you're probably where you belong. It's open daily from 10pm to about 5am.

Nihombashi & Ningyocho—Edo's First Commercial & Pleasure Centers

Start: Tokyo Station via the Marunouchi subway line or JR train such as the Yamanote Line, then Yaesu North Entrance exit.

Finish: Amazake Yokocho in Ningyocho. Station: Ningyocho.

Time: 4-5 hours, including stops along the way.

Best Times: Tuesday through Friday, when most shops and attractions are open. Start this tour around 10am, being sure to reach the Tokyo Stock Exchange before 3pm.

Worst Times: Monday, when most museums are closed; weekends, when the Tokyo Stock Exchange and the prefectural tourist shops in the Kokusai Kanko Kaikan and Daimaru are closed; Sunday, when smaller shops are closed.

When Ieyasu Tokugawa set up his shogunate in Edo back in the early 1600s, merchants and craftsmen from throughout Japan swarmed to the new city to serve the needs of the shogun, the resident feudal lords, and their samurai. It was here, in Nihombashi, located to the east of Edo Castle, that the first merchants settled, making it the commercial center of the city and therefore of all of Japan. Edo's city market was here, spread along the banks beside the Nihombashi Bridge, Japan's most important bridge and the starting point of all main highways leading out of the city to the provinces. Nihombashi was also home of Japan's first department stores, opened more than a century ago, and the city's main banks. Today Nihombashi serves as Tokyo's financial center, with the Tokyo Stock Exchange, the Bank of Japan, and the headquarters of major companies, several of whom operate small but important private museums.

Where merchants worked and lived, pleasure was never far away. Just east of Nihombashi, in a district called Ningyocho, Edo's first licensed pleasure quarter opened in 1617. In addition to brothels, it also boasted Kabuki theaters, puppet theaters, and traditional shops selling souvenirs and gifts. After a huge fire destroyed Ningyocho in 1657, the pleasure quarter was moved to Yoshiwara in the far outskirts of the city. Ningyocho has managed to retain some of its old Edo charm, especially along Amazake Yokocho, a picturesque street famous for several shops that have changed little over the decades. Together, Nihombashi and Ningyocho give insight into the Edo of yesterday and the Tokyo of today, with a number of things to see and do along the way. In my opinion, it's the diversity of this stroll that makes it one of the most interesting walks in the city.

• • • • • • • • • • • • • •

If you arrive at Tokyo Station via the Marunouchi Line, take the long passageway that runs underneath the station to the other side and exit from the Yaesu North Entrance. Likewise, if you arrive on one of the JR trains, follow the signs to the Yaesu North Entrance. In any case, be prepared to get lost, since this is:

1. **Tokyo Station,** Tokyo's main train station with more than 3,000 trains passing through daily. It serves as the nucleus for transportation throughout Japan, including Shinkansen bullet trains to Kyoto and Kyushu, long-distance trains, and commuter lines. Its Marunouchi side (west side) was completed in 1914 in red-brick and stone renaissance style, while the nondescript Yaesu side was completed in 1954. Incidentally, two prime ministers have been assassinated here by rival Japanese factions, in 1921 and 1930.

   Upon emerging from the Yaesu North Entrance exit, you will find yourself in a small square with a clock and, to your left, the Hotel Kokusai Kanko. At the clock, turn left and enter into the office building straight ahead, where you will see the prefectural office for Gunma. This is the:

2. **Kokusai Kanko Kaikan,** 1-8 Marunouchi (tel. 3215-1181), which doesn't look like much from the outside but is unique in Japan for its shopping opportunities. It, together with the ninth floor of the:

3. **Daimaru department store** located across the square, contain tourism promotional offices for every prefecture in Japan—each of which also sells its own special goods and products. Altogether there are 49 of these little shops, spread mainly on the second, third, and fourth floors of the Kokusai Kanko Kaikan building and the ninth floor of Daimaru. You won't find a more varied collection anywhere else in Japan; and prices are very reasonable, lower than at department stores. What's more, hardly anyone ever seems to shop here, so you don't have to deal with the crowds that plague other stores. Shop for Bizen pottery from Okayama, clay ningyo dolls from Fukuoka, noren (shop curtains) from Tochigo, or coral jewelry from Okinawa. Lacquerware, pottery, glassware, paper products, sake, kokeshi dolls, bamboo ware, pearls, china, kites, teapots, masks, food products, and everything else each prefecture is famous for can be found right here. Each office also has tourist pamphlets, unfortunately mostly in Japanese. Most offices are open Monday to Friday from about 9 or 10am to 5 or 6pm.

   Outside again in the square, take any steps leading down underground and head for Yaesu Central. This is the start of the:

Nihombashi & Ningyocho

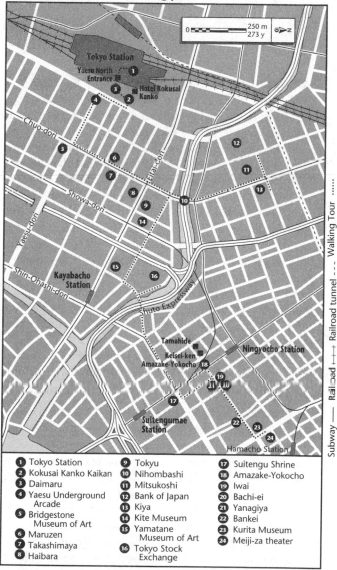

0 [scale bar] 250 m
273 y

Tokyo Station
Yaesu North Entrance
Hotel Kokusai Kanko
Chuo-dori
Harai-dori
Showa-dori
Yaesu-dori
Shin-Ohashi-dori
Kayabacho Station
Shuto Expressway
Tamahide
Keisei-ken
Amazake-Yokocho
Ningyocho Station
Suitengumae Station
Hamacho Station

Subway —— Railroad ┼┼┼ Railroad tunnel --- Walking Tour ......

1 Tokyo Station
2 Kokusai Kanko Kaikan
3 Daimaru
4 Yaesu Underground Arcade
5 Bridgestone Museum of Art
6 Maruzen
7 Takashimaya
8 Haibara
9 Tokyu
10 Nihombashi
11 Mitsukoshi
12 Bank of Japan
13 Kiya
14 Kite Museum
15 Yamatane Museum of Art
16 Tokyo Stock Exchange
17 Suitengu Shrine
18 Amazake-Yokocho
19 Iwai
20 Bachi-ei
21 Yanagiya
22 Bankei
23 Kurita Museum
24 Meiji-za theater

9702

4. Yaesu Underground Arcade, a long passageway lined on both sides with shops and eating establishments catering to commuters and those who work in the vicinity. Walk east through the huge underground shopping arcade, away from Tokyo Station and heading for Chuo-dori and signs that read KYOBASHI & NIHOMBASHI. Follow the arcade east to where it ends, turn right, and emerge above ground. On the corner of this busy road, Chuo-dori, is a modern black building, home of the:

5. **Bridgestone Museum of Art,** 1-10-1 Kyobashi (tel. 3563-0241). This private museum shows mainly European modern art, donated by the founder of the Bridgestone tire company (who, by the way, got his start by producing rubber soles for shoes worn by laborers). Open every day except Monday from 10am to 5:30pm and charging admission, the museum's permanent collection focuses on French Impressionists, with a few works by Manet, Monet, Degas, Sisley, Cézanne, Renoir, Pissarro, and Corot, and European paintings from the late 19th to the early 20th century, including works by Gauguin, Van Gogh, Matisse, Picasso, Modigliani, Utrillo, and Rousseau. It also contains modern Japanese Western-style art from the Meiji period onward, with works by Seiki Kuroda, Chu Asai, Shigeru Aoki, and Takeji Fujishima. Strangely enough, the museum also contains a room of ancient Egyptian, Greek, and Roman vases and sculptures.

Take a left out of the museum and return to Chuo-dori, where you should turn right. After one city block you'll see to your left:

6. **Maruzen,** 2-3-10 Nihombashi (tel. 3272-7211), which along with Kinokunia Bookstore in Shinjuku is Tokyo's most well-known bookstore. Founded in 1869 with the aim of introducing Western works to Japan, it has a large selection of foreign books on the second floor, including all the latest books concerning Japan and things Japanese. Go ahead and browse—standing and reading in a bookstore is so common that it could almost be called a national pastime. There's even a word for it, *tachiyomi,* which literally means "standing reading." While bookstore owners may lament such a custom, they nevertheless seem resigned to the practice, perhaps inevitable in a country where literacy is almost 100 percent and in a nation with one of the world's largest number of weekly and monthly publications. Besides, the Japanese are used to standing, whether it's in the subway, in a bus queue, or in a standup noodle shop. Reading in a

bookstore is a good way to pass the time waiting for the next appointment or for the next train home.

On the fourth floor of Maruzen is the Craft Center Japan, a small room that features changing exhibits of contemporary craftsmen and designers and traditional products. You might find glassware, ceramics, jewelry, chopsticks, and other items on display—I picked up some great cast-iron paperweights and bottle openers on my last visit, inexpensive but unique gifts. Maruzen is open Monday through Saturday from 10am to 6pm and on holidays from 10am to 6pm.

Across the street is:

7. **Takashimaya,** 2-4-1 Nihombashi (tel. 3211-4111), one of Tokyo's most attractive department stores. Founded as a kimono shop in Kyoto during the Edo Period and opening in Tokyo in 1933, it features boutiques by Louis Vuitton, Chanel, Hermes, Cartier, Fendi, Gucci, Issey Miyake, Kenzo, and Thierry Mugler and is famous for its kimono department on the third floor. It also has a good tableware department with beautiful selections of china and lacquerware. It's open every day except Wednesday from 10am to 7pm.

Take a Break There are a number of dining possibilities on the sixth floor of the **Takashimaya Annex,** from Chinese to tempura and udon noodles. Plastic display cases show reasonably priced set meals and other dishes, offered every day except Wednesday from 11am to 6pm.

One block farther north on Chuo-dori brings you to a large street, Eitai-dori, where you should turn right. In the middle of the block on the right-hand side is:

8. **Haibara (はいばら),** 2-7-6 Nihombashi (tel. 3272-3801), purveyors of Japanese paper since 1806. In addition, it sells fans, calligraphy paper, address books, cards, and stationery. It's open Monday through Saturday from 9:30am to 5:30pm.

Across the street is:

9. **Tokyu department store,** 1-4-1 Nihombashi (tel. 3273-3111), another chain of well-known Japanese department

stores. It's open every day except Thursday from 10am to 7pm.

Another block north on Chuo-dori brings you to:

10. **Nihombashi,** which means "Bridge of Japan" and, historically speaking, is the most important bridge in the nation. First built in 1603 as an arched wooden bridge, it was designated by Ieyasu Tokugawa as the starting point of all highways leading out of Edo and the spot from which distances to all other cities were measured. A bustling center in old Edo, the bridge and its banks served a number of communal functions, similar to a town square in medieval Europe. Public notices were posted here, and for a time, criminals were brought here for public display, both for ridicule and as a deterrent against similarly bad behavior. Edo's city market was also held here along the banks until the Great Kanto Earthquake of 1923, after which it was moved to Tsukiji. Rickshaws originated here in 1869, produced at a workshop at the foot of the bridge (the word "rickshaw," by the way, stems from a Japanese word *jinricksha,* which means "people-powered vehicle"). Four years later there were 34,000 rickshaws in Tokyo and they remained a popular form of transportation up until World War II. The present bridge, constructed in 1911 in Renaissance style, seems sadly neglected today, completely overshadowed by a noisy expressway that stretches unceremoniously right over it. The murky river below, once so clear that the third shogun, Iemitsu, swam it in as a boy, looks like it would cause instant death if you fell in. On the left-hand side of the bridge is a memorial to the original wooden arched bridge; on the other side is a marker designating the beginning point for measuring distances to other cities.

After crossing the bridge and the intersection to the north, you will see, to your left:

11. **Mitsukoshi department store,** 1-4-1 Nihombashi Muromachi (tel. 3241-3311), with its beautiful and stately Renaissance-style facade and an entrance guarded by two bronze lions, replicas of the lions in Trafalgar Square. One of Japan's oldest department stores, it was founded in 1673 by the Mitsui family as a dry goods store and claims many firsts in its long history. In 1683 it became the first store in

the world to deal only in cash sales and was also one of the first in Japan to begin displaying goods on shelves rather than having merchants fetch bolts of cloth for each customer, as was the custom at the time. It was also one of the first shops to employ female clerks. Today, with the imperial family and many visiting royalty among its customers, it boasts many name-brand boutiques, a well-known kimono department, and an art gallery. Look for bargain sales on the seventh floor. It's open from 10am to 6:30am, closed on Monday.

If architecture is one of your interests, turn left after Mitsukoshi and walk one block. To your right is the:

12. **Bank of Japan,** presently under renovation. Serving as the central bank of Japan, it was built in 1896 as Japan's first full-scale Western architectural work, in a neo-baroque style.

Back on Chuo-dori, look across the street for a sign that reads "World's First Cutlery." It marks the entrance to:

13. **Kiya,** 1-5-6 Nihombashi Muromachi (tel. 3241-0110), which opened in 1792 and specializes in custom-made knives and scissors. Everything from fingernail scissors to kitchen knives and ikebana scissors are for sale here. It's open Monday to Saturday from 10am to 6pm and Sunday and holidays from 11:30am to 5:30pm.

Take a left out of the store and walk back in the direction of Nihombashi Bridge. To your left is one of Edo's oldest neighborhoods, though of course you can't tell by looking at it today. One of its earliest and most famous residents was William Adams, the first Englishman ever to set foot on Japanese shores. Chief pilot on board a Dutch ship that wrecked off the coast of Kyushu in 1600, Adams was brought before Ieyasu Tokugawa, who quickly recognized the foreigner's potential and ordered him to remain in Japan to instruct him in ship building, gunnery, and navigation. Adams remained in Japan the rest of his life, marrying a Japanese woman and taking the name Anjin Miura. Foreigners probably know him best, however, as the role model for James Clavell's epic novel, *Shōgun*.

Re-cross Nihombashi Bridge, turning left into the tiny one-way alley just before Tokyu department store. You will presently come to a small intersection; across the street is a brown, five-story building. On its fifth floor is the:

14. **Kite Museum,** 1-12-10 Nihombashi (tel. 3271-2465), a private collection of more than 3,000 kites jam-packed in a few small rooms. Mainly Japanese kites, they range from miniature kites the size of postage stamps to kites dating from the Taisho Period, some ornately decorated with Kabuki stars, samurai, and animals. There are even hand-painted kites by ukiyo-e master Hiroshige. The museum, which charges admission, is open Monday to Saturday from 11am to 5pm.

Take a Break On the ground floor of the same building that houses the Kite Museum and under the same management is **Tameikan (たいめいけん),** an old Western-style restaurant (tel. 3271-2465), open since 1931. Simple, inexpensive, and often crowded, it has an English menu listing such dishes as ramen noodles, fried prawns, hamburger steak, spaghetti, and beef stew. To Western eyes, however, the food looks Japanese; to Japanese it's Western. In other words, this restaurant serves the classic Japanese version of Western food and in that respect has probably changed little since it opened. Diners are usually given both chopsticks and silverware, as though even the restaurant itself isn't sure what it serves. A good place for a quick, cheap meal, it's open Monday through Saturday from 11am to 8pm.

Turn left out of the museum and walk to busy Eitai-dori. Turn left here, crossing Showa-dori and walking underneath the Shuto Expressway. Presently to the left is the:

15. **Yamatane Museum of Art,** 7-12 Nihombashi Kabutocho (tel. 3669-7643), up on the seventh floor. Its collection of modern Japanese paintings includes works by Seiho Takeuchi (look for his *Spotted Cat*), Kagaku Murakami (*Woman in the Nude*), Kokei Kobayashi, and Togyu Oku-mura. It's open every day except Monday from 10am to 5pm and admission is charged.

If you've had enough sightseeing for the day, there's the Kayabacho subway station here in front of the museum.

Otherwise, take a left out of the museum and then the first left. Just before the overhead expressway is the:

16. **Tokyo Stock Exchange,** 2-1 Nihombashi-Kabutocho (tel. 3666-0141), with the visitors' entrance on the west (left) side of the building (follow the signs in English). Established in 1878, the Tokyo Stock Exchange vies with that of New York as one of the busiest in the world and has a great visitors' center, with a glass-enclosed observation deck from which to watch the frenetic activity on the trading floor. In addition, an excellent learning center called the Exhibition Plaza has a number of audiovisual displays to enhance the visitor's knowledge of securities and the stock market, with explanations in English. A three-dimensional display, for example, explains the intricacies of what takes place on the trading floor, while a robot demonstrates the various hand signals used by the traders. Computers simulate the actual experience of investing in stock by leading the visitor through various procedures. On the ground floor is a history hall tracing the development of the Japanese securities market. Back in the 19th century, for example, tatami were used instead of tables, and trading hours were determined by the amount of time it took for a certain length of rope to burn to the end. Admission to the visitors' center is free, and it's open Monday to Friday from 9am to 4pm. Note that trading hours, however, are from 9 to 11am and 12:30 to 3pm.

Take a right out of the visitors' center and then another right, walking alongside the Stock Exchange building. At the light, turn left and walk under the expressway and over the bridge. Continue walking in the same direction (east) on Shin-Ohashi-dori for about five minutes, until on your right you'll see the Suitengumae subway signs and the colorful oranges of:

17. **Suitengu Shrine,** with its entrance to the right up a flight of stairs. It's a favorite shrine for expectant mothers, who come to pray for a safe and easy delivery. According to legend, the shrine received its special status following a tragedy back in the 12th century, when a six-year-old emperor and his mother were forced to leap into the sea to escape

capture by their arch enemies, the Heike clan. Since then, the child and the sea have come to symbolize pregnancy and birth, and women traditionally visit the shrine during their fifth month when they begin to show, to buy a white cloth consecrated here and worn around their abdomen for protection. Since the white sash is generally worn with ki-mono, women buy it today just for good luck. Or perhaps you'll see grandparents here, buying the white sash for their future grandchild and praying for a safe delivery. Note how worshippers ring the five bells in front of the shrine to call attention to their prayers. In front of the shrine is also a statue of a dog with her puppy—touching the ball between the dog's front paws is thought to bring good luck, since dogs are generally thought to give birth easily.

Take a right out of the shrine, cross Shin-Ohashi-dori and walk north in the direction of the Ningyocho subway station, passing several maternity shops. After two short blocks you'll reach:

18. **Amazake-Yokocho,** a picturesque street lined with trees and traditional shops. This part of Ningyocho was left vir-tually untouched by the fire bombings of World War II, with architecture that dates back to the Showa Period with plaster-and-lath or wooden facades. A few even boast cop-per plating on their facades. To the left on Amazake Yokocho are a couple of refueling spots (see "Take a Break," below). For now, however, turn right, and after one short block on the corner to your left is a fascinating shop:

19. **Iwai,** 2-10-1 Ningyocho, a one-room workshop with a raised tatami floor where a craftsman sits to create beautiful lacquered bamboo boxes, adorned with family crests. In the olden days, such baskets were used to store kimono and other traditional Japanese clothes to protect them from mildew. Now that most Japanese have dressers, this shop is one of the last such workshops in the country. It's open every day except Sunday from 8:30am to 7:30pm.

Practically next door is another old shop:

20. **Bachi-ei (ばち英),** 2-10-11 Ningyocho, a tiny shop that makes the three-stringed samisen. The front display case

contains one of its instruments, along with a photograph showing the shop as it used to look decades ago. It's open every day except Sunday from 8am to 8pm.

Across the street is:

21. **Yanagiya (柳屋),** 2-11-3 Ningyocho (tel. 3666-9901), which has been turning out *tai-yaki*, bean-jam pastry in the shape of a fish, for more than 60 years. It boasts so many addicted customers that there's usually a queue here, lined up at the counter and open kitchen. Watch how the man whose job it is to fill the pastry works with a distinct rhythm—it's obvious he's been doing his job for a long time. The shop is open Monday to Saturday from 12:30 to 6pm.

Continue walking east on Amazake Yokocho until you come to a tree-lined median and a statue on your right of:

22. **Benkei,** a famous Kabuki actor and depicted here in a classical pose. The statue serves as a reminder that this area once boasted a number of Kabuki and puppet theaters.

Just beyond the statue, in a modern brown brick building on the left-hand side of Amazake Yokocho before the large intersection, is the:

23. **Kurita Museum,** 2-17-9 Nihombashi-Hamacho (tel. 3666-6242). Take the first entrance you come to and walk up the stairs. There are only a few rooms to this museum, but it contains an excellent display of exquisitely made Imari, Nabeshima, and Kakiemon porcelain, some of it 300 years old but as brilliantly colored as though it was produced only yesterday. The museum's founder and director, Hideo Kurita, arranged the museum to his own taste and even designed the building that houses it. Even more of his private collection of Imari and Nabeshima ware is on display at the much larger Kurita Museum in Ashikaga City. The Tokyo museum is open daily from 9:30am to 5pm and admission is charged.

Across the busy street is the massive building housing the:

24. **Meiji-za theater,** with its posters outside advertising the current program, often Kabuki and traditional plays. It was founded in 1893 as the first theater in Japan to boast

electric lighting. On a tragic note, thousands of people died here during a 1945 bombing raid, after taking refuge inside the theater which subsequently went up in flames.

If you continue walking straight, you'll come to Hamacho subway station. Or, return to the main intersection of Amazake Yokocho near the traditional shops listed above, where you'll find the Ningyocho subway station for the Hibiya Line.

Take a Break Keisei-ken, 1-17-9 Ningyocho (tel. 3661-3855), is a small coffeeshop on Amazake Yokocho that first opened in 1919 as one of Tokyo's first western-style teahouses selling British tea rather than the traditional Japanese tea. It's been remodeled since then but certainly not in the past few decades, leaving it with an old-fashioned and slightly corny atmosphere reminiscent of the '50s or '60s. It's open every day except Sunday from 7am to 7pm. Just past Keisei-ken is one of Ningyocho's most well-known restaurants, **Tamahide (玉ひで),** 1-17-10 Ningyocho (tel. 3668-7651), founded in 1760 and serving only chicken dishes. It offers an inexpensive lunch of chicken and rice from 11:30am to 1pm; dinner, available from 4 to 9pm, features much more expensive set courses. The restaurant is located in a traditional white mortar building; look for its display windows complete with live chickens in a case located near the Keisei-ken coffee shop. The restaurant is closed on Sundays.

Yanaka—Temple Town

Start: Tennoji Temple. Station: Nippori, then the north exit.

Finish: Nezu Temple. Station: Nezu.

Time: Allow approximately four hours, including stops along the way.

Best Times: There is no "best" time, as such, for this walk.

Worst Times: Monday and Friday, when museums are closed.

Yanaka has been a temple town ever since the Edo Period, when most temples and shrines were removed from the inner city and relocated to the outskirts in an attempt to curb the frequent fires that ravaged the crowded shogunate capital. Not only did the religious structures' thatched roofs ignite like tinder, but the land they formerly occupied could subsequently be cleared and left empty, to act as firebreaks in the otherwise densely populated city. Furthermore, temples on the edge of town could double as forts to protect Edo from invasion. The only invasions Yanaka suffered, however, were friendly ones, as townspeople flocked here to enjoy its peacefulness, wooded hills, paddies, clear streams, and majestic temple compounds. It wasn't long before the wealthy began building country estates here, followed by artists and writers who favored Yanaka's picturesque setting and cool breezes.

Today Yanaka still boasts Tokyo's greatest concentration of temples, most dating from the Edo Period. It's also largely residential, with narrow lanes, old houses, and a few unique museums and traditional shops tucked here and there among the gently sloping hills. Because there are no major attractions or department stores here, the atmosphere of this stroll is markedly different from the bustling liveliness of the other strolls—there are no crowds and there's very little traffic. Rather, a trip to Yanaka is like visiting a small town, where the pace of life is slow and the people have time for each other. If Tokyo is starting to wear on your nerves, come here to refresh yourself.

• • • • • • • • • • • • • • • • •

Probably the easiest way to get to Yanaka is on the Yamanote Line. Disembark at Nippori Station, exiting at the north end of the platform (the end closest to Nishi-Nippori Station) and turning left. Look for the flight of steps up the hill, beside the public telephones and a map of the area. Walk through the cemetery, following the footpath until it joins a paved road. Ahead and to the left is the first temple on our tour:

1. **Tennoji Temple,** founded more than 500 years ago. It used to be a grand and impressive complex, 10 times its present size and popular among townspeople as one of Edo's three temples authorized to hold lotteries. The lotteries, however, drew such huge crowds and got so out of hand that they were banned in the mid-19th century by the Tokugawa shogunate. Then, in 1868, most of the complex was destroyed in the battle between the Tokugawa loyalists and Imperial forces on nearby Ueno Hill. Today, Tennoji is quiet and peaceful, with neatly swept grounds and the soothing sounds of chirping birds and chanting monks. The first thing you see upon entering the compound is a seated bronze Buddha, dating from 1690 and one of the temple's dearest treasures. Nearby is a standing *jizo,* guardian of children's spirits. This one was erected by a grieving father more than 60 years ago, following the death of his son in a playground accident.

Walk out of the temple compound's main entrance and continue walking straight through:

Yanaka—Temple Town

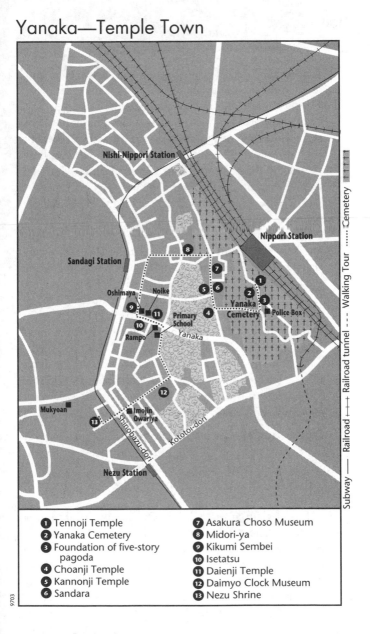

Subway — Railroad ┼┼┼ Railroad tunnel - - - Walking Tour ⋯⋯ Cemetery ┼┼┼┼┼

1. Tennoji Temple
2. Yanaka Cemetery
3. Foundation of five-story pagoda
4. Choanji Temple
5. Kannonji Temple
6. Sandara
7. Asakura Choso Museum
8. Midori-ya
9. Kikumi Sembei
10. Isetatsu
11. Daienji Temple
12. Daimyo Clock Museum
13. Nezu Shrine

2. **Yanaka Cemetery,** once the burial grounds of Kanei-ji and Tennoji temples and opened to the public in 1874. As one of Tokyo's largest cemeteries, it has more than 7,000 tombstones, including graves belonging to famous public figures, artists, and writers, some of whom lived in the area.

Among the most famous writers buried here are Soseki Natsume (1867–1916) and Ogai Mori (1862–1922), both novelists of the Meiji era and longtime Yanaka residents. Natsume, whose portrait is featured on the 1,000-yen note, became famous after writing *I Am a Cat,* a humorous look at the follies of human society as seen through the eyes of a cat. Ogai, who at 19 was the youngest graduate ever from the medical school at Tokyo University and who later became surgeon general, was a foremost figure of modern Japanese literature, with works that tried to bridge the gap between the traditional and the modern, as Japan moved away from its feudal agrarian past and plunged headlong into its role as an industrialized nation. Today the cemetery is quite peaceful and empty, but it wasn't always so. During the Edo Period, teahouses along its edge served more than tea, with monks among their frequent customers. One of the teahouse beauties, Osen Kasamori, achieved fame when ukiyo-e master Harunobu immortalized her in several of his works.

In a minute or two you'll come to two very strange sights in a cemetery—a police box and a children's playground. Here, between the two and surrounded by a low bamboo fence and hedge, is the:

3. **foundation of a five-story pagoda.** First built in 1644 but burned down in 1772, it was reconstructed as the tallest pagoda in Edo. It met its final demise in 1957, when it was burned down by two lovers who then committed suicide.

Take a right at the police box and walk straight into a residential street, following it until it ends at a T-intersection. Ahead is a plaque marking the tomb of Hogai Kano (1828–1888), a Japanese painter of the early Meiji Period who incorporated western techniques in his work and, along with Tenshin Okakura, is credited for "modernizing" Japanese art. Behind the plaque is:

4. **Choanji Temple,** dedicated to the god of longevity, one of Japan's seven lucky gods. During the Edo Period, a pilgrimage to all seven temples, each housing one of the seven gods of fortune, was thought to bring good luck. Now that such pilgrimages have lost their appeal, Choanji seems rather forgotten. In addition to Kano's tomb, the temple is

notable for its three stone stupas dating from the 1200s. They are located straight ahead on the main path, at the end to the left by the statues.

Turn left out of Choanji. Presently, to your left, will be:

5. **Kannonji Temple.** A small pagoda to the right of its front entrance is dedicated to the 47 ronin, masterless samurai who avenged their master's death and then committed ritual suicide in 1702. Capturing the public's imagination, their story has become a popular Kabuki play. Two of the ronin were brothers of a head priest here.

A stone's throw farther north, on the right, is:

6. **Sandara (さんだら工芸),** 7-18-6 Yanaka (tel. 5814-8618), a small crafts shop selling pottery and baskets. Open every day except Monday from 10am to 6pm, it takes its name from sacks once used to hold rice.

Past this shop, also on the right, is one of the highlights of this stroll, the:

7. **Asakura Choso Museum,** 7-18-10 Yanaka (tel. 3821-4549). With its modern black facade, it looks rather out of place in this traditional neighborhood, but its interior is a delightful mix of modern and traditional architecture and is one of Tokyo's most intriguing homes open to the public. Built in 1936, it was the home and studio of Fumio Asakura (1888–1964) a Western-style sculptor known for his realistic statues of statesmen, women, and—cats (a lover of felines, Asakura once had as many as a dozen cats running around his studio, which he used as models). After passing through his studio with its soaring ceilings, you'll find yourself in a traditional Japanese house, which wraps itself around an inner courtyard pond. There's even a rooftop garden. On display are several of his kimono, which he much preferred over western-style dress. The admission is well worth the price to see this beautiful house, open from 9:30am to 4:30pm, closed Monday and Friday.

Take a right out of the museum, turning left at the next street (if you take a right here, you will end up back at Nippori Station). Keep to the right and walk down the steps. Then take the first right, located just past the arched entryway marking the neighborhood's pedestrian-only shopping lane. Here, to your right, is:

8. **Midori-ya（竹芸）,** 3-13-5 Nishi-Nippori (tel. 3828-1746), an exquisite basket shop with several samples on display outside its front door. It's the store and workshop of Suigetsu Buseki and his son Sui Koh, a charming father-and-son team who coax flexible strands of bamboo into beautifully crafted baskets, some of them signed. With the Imperial family and visiting dignitaries among its customers, including a former U.S. ambassador to Japan, the shop is known for its use of smoked bamboo, taken from the underside of thatched farmhouses and exhibiting a beautiful gloss and subtle color gradation attained from years of indoor fire pits. As such antique pieces of bamboo are increasingly hard to come by, some of the baskets here are rightfully expensive, but are still less expensive than what they fetch at major department stores. Freshly cut bamboo is also used for some of the less expensive pieces. You can linger here, and with customers that speak Japanese, the Busekis are happy to discuss their trade and their love, as though they had nothing better to do than spend time talking with anyone who happens by their shop, open daily from 9am to 7pm.

Retrace your steps to the corner and turn right onto the shopping lane, pleasant because it's free from cars and, unlike many shopping streets nowadays, isn't a covered arcade. Look for the tofu shop, a must in any Japanese neighborhood. At the end of the shopping street, turn left and walk about five minutes, passing the Sendagi business hotel on the way, until you come to a stoplight and a slightly larger road.

Take a Break Immediately to the left of the stoplight, on the corner, is a noodle shop called **Oshimaya （大島屋）,** 3-2-5 Yanaka (tel. 3821-5052). It's located on the second floor of a modern building but has traditional touches of bamboo screens at the window and an indoor pond with fish. Open every day except Friday from 11am to 8pm, it offers two different kinds of noodles—soba and udon—served in a variety of ways, including tempura soba, sansai udon (with mountain vegetables), and tanuki soba (cold noodles served with vegetables, seaweed, crab and egg). Practically next door is **Noike （乃池）,** 3-2-3 Yanaka (tel. 3821-3922), a small sushi shop with flower boxes outside its front door. Its specialty is anagozushi, grilled conger eel, but it also has tuna, mackerel, shrimp, and all the other usual sushi offerings. Closed on Tuesdays, it's open the rest of the week from 11:30am to 2pm and 4:30 to 10pm, except on Sundays when it stays open from 11:30am to 8pm. If all you want is a drink, farther down the street on the right-hand side is **Rampo (乱歩),** 2-9-14 Yanaka (tel. 3828-9494), a coffee shop offering soft drinks, coffee, and tea and open every day except Monday from 10am to 7pm. Look for the wooden "Coffee Snack" sign above its door.

If you take a right at the stoplight, to your right you will soon see:

9. **Kikumi Sembei (菊見せんべい),** 3-37-16 Sendagi (tel. 3821-1215). You can't miss it—look for the beautiful, 110-year-old wooden building, with its traditional open-fronted shop selling Japanese crackers. Open every day except Monday from 10am to 7pm, it's definitely worth a photograph. You might even want to buy some of its square-shaped sembei.

Just beyond the cracker shop is Sendagi Station. Unless you're ready to call it quits, however, turn around and head back in the opposite direction, passing the stoplight and the two restaurants listed above. On your right, on a corner, is:

10. **Isetatsu (いせ辰),** 2-18-9 Yanaka (tel. 3823-1453), a crafts store that sells items made from Japanese paper, including paper fans, papier-mâché objects, and boxes. Founded in the mid-1800s and run by the Hirose family for four generations, it specializes in *chiyogami,* handmade decorative paper printed with wood blocks. Some of the designs are the family's own creations; others are taken from family crests used by samurai and members of the court and worn on kimono and armor. The most expensive papers are rare and cannot be reproduced. It's open daily from 10am to 6pm.

Continuing in the same direction (east), in the next block on the left side is:

11. **Daienji Temple,** 3-1-2 Yanaka, located opposite the grade school. This temple honors ukiyo-e master Harunobu, one

of Edo's most famous artists, and Osen Kasamori, who worked at one of the many teahouses near Tennoji in the 1760s and achieved fame when Harunobu singled her out as a model for many of his portraits. The larger stone marker is a monument to Harunobu; the smaller one to the left is Osen's.

Cross back to the other side of the street at the cross walk, turn left, and then take the first right after the elementary school. Turn left at the end of the street, and presently, to your right, will be the:

12. **Daimyo Clock Museum** (Daimyo Tokei Haku-butsukan), 2-1-27 Yanaka (tel. 3821-6913), with its one-room display of clocks and watches of the Edo Period (1603–1867). About 50 examples from the museum's extensive collection are on display at any one time, with exhibitions changed annually, and range from huge freestanding clocks to sundials, alarm clocks, pocket watches, and small watches that were attached to obi (the sash worn with a kimono). The first clock was brought to Japan by a missionary in the 16th century, and in typical Japanese fashion, was quickly modified to suit local needs. Rather than measuring 24 hours a day, Edo clocks were based on the length of time between sunrise and sunset, so that time varied greatly with the seasons. Clocks, which had to be set once or twice a day, were so expensive that only daimyo, or feudal lords, could afford them. Most daimyo had both a clock maker and clock setter under their employ, since castles were large and generally contained several huge clocks on their grounds. Apparently, time was of the essence in Japan even back then. Unfortunately, explanations in the museum are in Japanese only, and admission is charged. It's open from 10am to 4pm, closed on Monday, the months of July, August, and September, and from December 25 to January 14.

Take a left out of the clock museum and then the first left (note the weirdly shaped pine tree on the corner), and walk down one of the many slopes for which Yanaka is famous and which still have some traditional wooden homes. On the left-hand side of the slope, at the bottom just before the stoplight, is Imojin Owariya, a Japanese sweet shop (see "Final Take a Break," below). Cross the busy street, Shinobazu-dori, at the stoplight and continue straight. The road will begin to slope upwards, and then, to your right, will be:

13. **Nezu Shrine,** one of Tokyo's best-kept secrets. With its brightly colored oranges, venerable cedars, and manicured azalea bushes, it's a welcome contrast to the austerity of the Buddhist temples that dominate Yanaka. It was built in 1706 by the fifth Tokugawa shogun and features a front court-yard gate of red lacquer with joists in gilt, green, blue, or-ange, and black. Take a rest here on the shrine's serene grounds.

   To reach Nezu Station, return to Shinobazu-dori and turn right.

   Take a Break   On the slope up from Shinobazu-dori in the direction of the clock museum is **Imojin Owariya (尾張屋)**, 2-30-4 Nezu (tel. 3821-5530), a tiny, old shop selling Japanese sweets and ice cream. Look for the small display case outside its front door. Inside it's very plain, with just a few tables, kind of like a Japanese version of a small-town ice cream parlor. It sells home-made ice cream, either vanilla or sweet bean, as well as shaved ice with flavorings of sweet bean paste, lemon, strawberry, or melon. It's open daily from 11am to about 8pm. For something a bit more substantial, there's a noodle shop not far from Nezu Shrine (to reach it, take the back exit from Nezu Shrine and then turn left; it's up the hill, to your left). Housed in a traditional Japanese house with a small garden in back, **Mikyoan (夢境庵)**, 1-6-4 Yayoi (tel. 3815-4337), serves some of the city's best hand-made soba and is open every day except Friday from 10am to 7pm.

AKASAKA—
BUSINESSMAN'S TOKYO

Start: National Diet Building, Nagatacho. Station: Kokkaigijido-Mae, then exit 1 for the National Diet Building.

Finish: Akasaka Prince Hotel. Station: Nagatacho or Akasaka-Mitsuke.

Time: Allow approximately three hours, not including take a break stops.

Best Times: Late afternoon, when you can finish the tour with drinks and dinner in Akasaka's nightlife district. If the Suntory Museum of Art is a primary reason for taking this stroll, be sure to start at around 3pm so that you can reach the museum by 4:30. Otherwise, the best day for this tour is Friday, when the Suntory Museum of Art remains open until 7pm and Akasaka's nightlife is in full swing.

Worst Times: Sunday, when many restaurants in Akasaka are closed; Monday, when the Suntory Museum of Art is closed.

With the fall of the Tokugawa shogunate in 1868, Japan's feudal era came to an end. Under the skillful reign of Emperor Meiji, a prime minister and a cabinet were appointed, a constitution was drafted, and a parliament, called the Diet, was elected. Since Tokyo's financial and commercial centers were already firmly rooted east of the Imperial Palace in Hibiya and Nihombashi, the area immediately west of the palace was eventually chosen for its central location as the site of the nation's new administrative center. Called Kasumigaseki and formerly dotted with stately mansions belonging to feudal lords, it became home to the National Diet, the prime minister's office and residence, and various government offices.

Politicians, of course, need some place where they can entertain friends and woo enemies, and that, coupled with Japan's long history of nighttime diversions, made adjacent Akasaka a natural as an after-hours entertainment district. By the end of the 19th century, Akasaka boasted some of the city's most exclusive geisha houses, as well as a number of brothels and bars. Today Akasaka remains one of Tokyo's most sophisticated night spots, popular with politicians, bureaucrats, Japanese businessmen, and foreigners staying at one of Akasaka's several luxury hotels. A few of the city's most expensive entertainment houses remain, singular in their high, plain wooden walls and chauffeured limousines parked outside, the realm of those on unlimited expense accounts. Most of Akasaka's establishments, however, are much more egalitarian, ablaze in neon and catering to those in search of a few drinks and dinner. There are also a few sightseeing attractions in Akasaka, including a shrine, an art museum, and a 400-year-old garden, making it a good place for a short stroll, especially if you're staying in one of the nearby hotels and have a few hours free. Since Akasaka is most well known as a night spot, try to time this walk for late afternoon, when you can top it off with a meal at one of Akasaka's restaurants.

● ● ● ● ● ● ● ● ● ● ● ● ● ● ●

We start this tour not in Akasaka but in adjoining Kasumigaseki, just a short walk away. You can reach Kokkaigijido-Mae station on either the Chiyoda or Marunouchi line, but in any case take exit 1, turning right out of the station and walking to the intersection. Catty-corner is the:

1. **prime minister's residence,** which has seen quite a bit of the moving vans in the past few years. Since it's surrounded by a wall and is under the constant surveillance of guards, all you can see of the residence is its brick exterior and tiled roof, from which waves the Japanese flag. No commute for the prime minister—his office is conveniently located right across the street.

   Turn right at the intersection, and after a minute's walk you'll come to the:

2. **National Diet Building** (Kokkai Gijido) on the right, home of Japan's parliament. Completed in 1936 after 17 years of construction and clearly influenced by western architecture, it is divided into the House of Representatives (the wing to the right) and the House of Councillors (on the left). The central hall, underneath the pyramid, is reserved for the emperor, who makes an official visit at the beginning of the first session as the nation's figurehead but who has no official role in the government. As the legislative body of the government, the Diet is elected by the people, with members of the House of Representatives serving four-year terms and members of the House of Councillors six-year terms. The major role of the House of Councillors is to re-examine decisions handed down by the House of Representatives. The prime minister, who is designated by the National Diet and must himself be a member of the Diet, has the power to dissolve the House of Representatives at any time.

   Facing away from the National Diet Building, cross the busy street at the crosswalk and stoplight and head west downhill in the direction of the Capitol Tokyu Hotel. After passing the streetlight, turn left and walk uphill toward the Capitol Tokyu, before which you will soon see a concrete torii and steps leading up to:

3. **Hie Shrine** with its typical Shinto architecture. Originally built inside the shogun's castle in the 15th century and moved to its present location in 1659, it was one of the most important shrines of Edo, honored by generations of Tokugawa shogun as home of the guardian god of Edo Castle and therefore of Edo itself. At the entrance to the shrine compound is a statue of a female monkey holding a baby

Akasaka—Businessman's Town

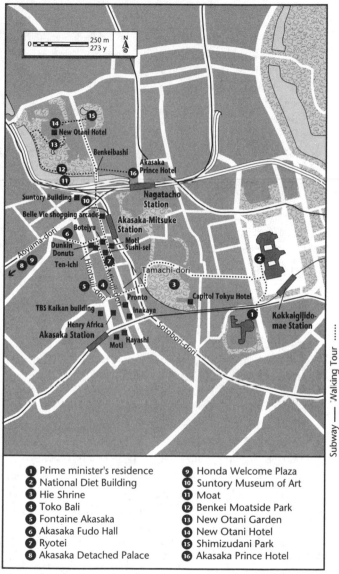

0 ——————— 250 m
273 y
N

14 New Otani Hotel
13
Benkeibashi
15
12
11
16 Akasaka Prince Hotel
Suntory Building 10
Nagatacho Station
Belle Vie shopping arcade
Akasaka-Mitsuke Station
Botejyu
6
Moti
Dunkin Donuts
Sushi-sei
7
Ten-ichi
Tamachi-dori
5 4
3
Pronto
Capitol Tokyu Hotel
TBS Kaikan building
Inakaya
1
Henry Africa
Kokkaigijidomae Station
Akasaka Station
Moti Hayashi
Aoyama-dori
Hitotsugi-dori
Mitsui-dori
Sotobori-dori

8 9

Subway —   Walking Tour ......

1 Prime minister's residence		**9** Honda Welcome Plaza
2 National Diet Building		**10** Suntory Museum of Art
3 Hie Shrine		**11** Moat
4 Toko Bali		**12** Benkei Moatside Park
5 Fontaine Akasaka		**13** New Otani Garden
6 Akasaka Fudo Hall		**14** New Otani Hotel
7 Ryotei		**15** Shimizudani Park
8 Akasaka Detached Palace		**16** Akasaka Prince Hotel

9704

monkey—the monkey serves as the messenger to the guardian god and is worshipped today for protection against miscarriage and as a symbol of marital harmony. The grounds are usually pleasantly empty, save for some roaming chickens and during the popular Sanno Festival held in mid-June. If you wish, you can find out your fortune in English—if you don't like what it says, simply negate it by tying the fortune slip to the rope at the front gate.

Exit the grounds by walking around the shrine to the right. In the back corner you'll see a row of densely packed orange torii leading downhill, a picturesque sight and a wonderfully cheerful epilogue to the shrine itself. At the bottom of the hill turn right, walk under the large concrete torii, and then cross busy Sotobori-dori and continue walking straight. After passing a small alley, you will quickly come upon Tamachi-dori, Misuji-dori, and Hitotsuji-dori in quick succession. These narrow lanes are the heart of Akasaka's nightlife district, with plenty of opportunities for eating and drinking. On the corner of Misuji-dori is one of the area's few tourist shops:

4. **Toko Bali,** 4-15-3 Akasaka (tel. 3583-2457), crammed full with Asian folk crafts, including clothing, textiles, jewelry, and knickknacks. It's open from 11am to 11pm, closed on Sundays.

Take a Break   For a quick and inexpensive pick-me-up, there's the **Pronto** coffee chain on Tamachi-dori at 3-12-1 Akasaka (tel. 3582-3717), open every day except Sunday from 8am to 11pm. Like others in its chain, it's a coffee house by day, changing into a bar after 5:30pm. Unfortunately, it can be quite smoky inside, but if weather permits try to get a seat at the outdoor table. Also on Tamachi-dori is the inexpensive **Botejyu (ぼてぢゅう)**, located above the Subway Shop at 3-10-1 Akasaka (tel. 3584-6651). Closed on Saturday but open the rest of the week from noon to 3pm and 5 to 10pm, it specializes in okonomiyaki, which is a Japanese-style pizza/pancake topped with cabbage and a meat such as pork, squid, or shrimp. It also serves fried noodles (yakisoba) and teppanyaki (grilled beef). On Hitotsugi-dori is the TBS Kaikan building, 5-3-3 Akasaka, with several well-known restaurants in its basement. **La Granata** offers two dining facilities here, both with the same menu and open every day from 11am to 9:30pm. The Ristorante (tel. 3582-3241) is the place to go for traditional Italian decor, with ochre-colored walls, wooden ceiling beams, and an open charcoal grill, while the Granata Moderna (tel. 3582-5891) features modern decor with an emphasis on art nouveau. Both offer lunch specials, available to 3pm, and pizza until 5pm, after which diners feast on pasta, seafood, and veal. Across the corridor is **Zakuro** (tel. 3582-6841), which bills itself as a "Japanese Folk Craft Restaurant" and features Kobe beef in its servings of shabu-shabu and sukiyaki. With its English menu, it's a popular dining choice for foreign business people. Across from the TBS Kaikan building, up on the second floor, is **Henry Africa,** one of the best places in the immediate vicinity for a mid-day cocktail or beer. It's open Monday to Friday from 11:30am to 11:30pm and on weekends from 5:30 to 10:30pm. There are two **Moti** restaurants in Akasaka, famous in Tokyo for its Indian cuisine. One is on Tamachi-dori at 3-8-8 Akasaka (tel. 3584-3760) and the other is across from the south end of Hitotsugi-dori at 2-14-31 Akasaka (tel. 3584-6640). Both are open daily from 11:30am to 10pm.

Turn right on Hitotsugi-dori and head north. Almost immediately to your left, on the corner, is a blue tiled building, the:

5. **Fontaine Akasaka,** 4-3-5 Akasaka (tel. 3583-6554), one of Tokyo's so-called capsule hotels. Like most capsule hotels, this one is for men only, mostly Japanese businessmen who have spent the evening drinking with fellow workers and have missed the last train home. Cheaper than a taxi ride to the suburbs, capsule hotels offer coffin-size units, usually stacked two deep along a long corridor and equipped with color TV, radio, and alarm clock. The only privacy is that afforded by a flimsy curtain, not much considering most inmates are probably inebriated. This hotel has a sauna, a public bath, no-smoking floors, and vending machines selling everything from beer and instant noodles to toothbrushes. Note the picture at the hotel's entrance showing a tattooed man being turned away—tattoos are associated with Japanese gangsters. The hotel's English brochure also admonishes, "Dead drunks are requested to keep out." The joys of Japanized English.

Continue walking north on Hitotsugi-dori, passing more shops, pachinko parlors, and karaoke bars.

Pachinko

It would be hard to walk around any town in Japan for too long without noticing the ubiquitous pachinko parlor. Usually brightly lit, garish, and noisy with the clanging of machines and lively background music, a pachinko parlor is packed with upright units similar to pinball machines, with row upon row of Japanese businessmen, housewives, and students sitting intently and quietly in front of them. Popular since the end of World War II as an inexpensive form of entertainment and named after the sound balls make when striking obstacles inside the machine, pachinko is a game in which ball bearings are flung into the machine, one after the other, with points amassed according to which holes the ball bearings fall into. Players control the strength with which the ball is released, but otherwise there's very little to do. Still, the Japanese contend it's a game of skill, with the payoff in more steel balls. These balls can be traded in for food, cigarettes, watches, calculators, and the like. It's illegal to win money in Japan, but outside many pachinko parlors, along back alleyways, are tiny windows where you can trade in what you won for cash. Everyone knows the windows are there; police just look the other way.

Near the north end of Hitotsugi-dori is a Dunkin' Donuts on the right-hand side. Opposite it, on the left side of Hitotsugi-dori, is a small orange torii marking the entrance to:

6. **Akasaka Fudo Hall.** Walk uphill, underneath the string of lanterns and past a small cemetery. The small shrine at the top of the hill offers fortunes in English, which you can obtain by shaking a bamboo container until a stick with a number falls out. Then, according to a sign in English which advises you to "ransack a drawer for same number," open the drawer that matches the number on your stick and withdraw the sheet of paper with English on it. If you don't like what it has to say, get rid of it by tying it to one of the nearby bushes.

Retrace your steps back down the hill, cross Hitotsugi-dori and walk straight past the Dunkin' Donuts shop, turning right on the next street, Misuji-dori. Soon, on your left, you'll see a tall wooden fence at 3-10 Akasaka, one of the district's expensive entertainment houses, called a:

7. **ryotei.** Ryotei restaurants are Japan's highest and most expensive class of restaurants, patronized by top executives and politicians on expense accounts. The architecture of such places is almost always austerely plain and traditional, and entertainment is provided by geisha who are trained in singing, playing the samisen, and traditional Japanese dance. Top-level entertainers, geisha train for years, following a rigorous schedule that few Japanese girls today are willing to undergo.

Turn left after the ryotei and walk one block to Tamachi-dori, where you should turn left again and walk north. To your right will be Akasaka-Mitsuke subway station and the Belle Vie shopping arcade, with six floors of boutiques selling clothing, handbags, jewelry, shoes, and other accessories appealing to middle-aged Japanese women. At the north end of Tamachi-dori is Aoyama-dori, which runs southwest from here through Aoyama to Shibuya.

If you have time and you're a fan of Honda automobiles, turn left here and walk in the direction of Aoyama. On your right you'll pass the extensive grounds belonging to the:

8. **Akasaka Detached Palace,** completed in 1909 as the residence of the Crown Prince. Emperor Taisho spent his honeymoon here when he was still Crown Prince. Inspired by 18th-century French architecture, the palace is lavishly decorated in neo-baroque fashion and today serves as Japan's official state guest house for visiting chiefs of state and is therefore not open to the public.

After passing the Canadian Embassy on your left, designed with slanting walls not unlike those of a Japanese castle, you will come to the Daien Higashi-dori and Aoyama-dori intersection. Here, on your left, is the:

9. **Honda Welcome Plaza,** 2-1-1 Minami-Aoyama (tel. 3423-4118), a showroom for the car company's latest models, many not yet available in the United States. It's

open weekdays from 9:30am to 6:30pm and weekends from 10am to 6pm.

A 10-minute walk will bring you back to where we were in Akasaka, where, on the corner of Aoyama-dori and Sotobori-dori, is the Suntory Building, which belongs to one of Japan's best-known brewing companies. Up on the 11th floor is the:

10. **Suntory Museum of Art** (Suntory Bijutsukan), 1-2-3 Moto-Akasaka (tel. 3470-1073), with its collection of ancient Japanese art, including paintings and screens, and items used in everyday life, ranging from clothing and furniture to lacquerware and eating utensils. Exhibitions change frequently, centering on certain themes. It's open every day except Monday and during exhibition changes from 10am to 5pm, except on Friday when it remains open until 7pm. Admission is charged.

Continue north, crossing the large busy street with the overhead expressway, to the Benkei-bashi bridge over the:

11. **moat.** With its sluggish brown water, it doesn't hold much of interest today, except perhaps to the few anglers who sometimes fish from the banks. During the Edo Period, this small body of water was part of a vast whorl of moats that circled outward from the shogun's castle, crossed by more than 30 bridges. Most of the moats have since been filled in, so that this is one of the few still remaining. Boats are for rent here in the warm summer months, but the experience looks about as enticing as swimming laps in a bathtub. Rather, right behind the boat house, turn left onto a shaded footpath, called the:

12. **Benkei Moatside Park,** which follows the rounded contour of the moat and offers a few benches for rest and contemplation. After about a five-minute walk, you'll come to a steep flight of stairs. Turn right at the top of the stairs and then right again onto the grounds of the New Otani Hotel, passing the hotel's swimming pool before arriving at the wonderful:

13. **New Otani Garden,** the most spectacular hotel garden in Tokyo. It was once the private grounds of Kiyomasa Kato, a famous feudal lord from Kumamoto, and one of many

estates that once dotted the Akasaka area during the shogun era. Today the 400-year-old garden sprawls over 10 acres of ponds, waterfalls, bridges, bamboo groves, and manicured bushes. Take an unhurried stroll here (entrance is free), ending up above the waterfall where some stairs lead into the:

14. **New Otani Hotel,** 4-1 Kioi-cho (tel. 3265-1111). With 1,800 rooms and suites, more than 30 restaurants and bars, a shopping arcade with more than a 100 stores, and even an art museum, the New Otani is like a small city, much too crowded and busy for my tastes. It's also easy to get lost here. Of interest to visitors, however, is the hotel's tea ceremony offered Thursdays, Fridays, and Saturdays from 11am to noon and 1 to 4pm. A fee is charged, and it's best to telephone beforehand to make a reservation (tel. 3265-1111).

Take a Break   Among the New Otani Hotel's many restaurants are **La Tour d'Argent** (tel. 3239-3111), one of Tokyo's most expensive French restaurants and open for dinner only from 5:30 to 9:30pm, and **Trader Vic's** (tel. 3265-4708), part of an American chain offering South Pacific inspired dishes daily from 11:30am to 2.30pm and 5 to 10pm. For a unique setting, try **Garden Barbecue** (tel. 3265-1111), a glass-enclosed teppanyaki restaurant located in the 400-year-old garden and open daily from noon to 2pm and 5 to 11pm. If all you want is a drink, head for the New Otani's **Garden Lounge,** which offers an afternoon tea and coffee with views over the garden. Try to get a window seat.

Exit the New Otani from its main entrance, near the reception desk. Walk through the parking lot and then turn right, walking downhill. Cross at the stoplight, and then turn right. Almost immediately on your left is:

15. **Shimizudani Park,** a very small oasis of green with a pond and mutantly huge carp and ravens.

Past the park, also on the left, is the:

16. **Akasaka Prince Hotel,** 1-2 Kioi-cho (tel. 3234-1111), the epitome of a Japanese luxury hotel with excellent service. A gleaming-white, 40-story skyscraper, it was designed

by Kenzo Tange, Japan's foremost architect who also designed the 1964 Olympic indoor stadium in Yoyogi and the new Tokyo Metropolitan Government office in Shinjuku. When the Akasaka Prince opened in 1983, it caused quite a stir, as some Tokyoites complained that it was too cold and sterile. In my opinion, however, the hotel, sensuously shaped like a Japanese folding fan, was simply ahead of its time. Japanese style, after all, has always called for simplicity, and this hotel's design projects that simplicity into the 21st century. Its lobby is intentionally spacious and empty, lined with almost 12,000 slabs of white marble, so as not to compete with the brilliant Japanese kimono. The bare, spacious look is now very much in vogue in Japan, and wedding receptions are held here so frequently that you may very well spot a wedding party in the lobby— the women will most likely be dressed in their finest kimono or designer Western dress, while men wear black suites and white ties. Japanese weddings are usually elaborate affairs, with sit-down dinners for hundreds of guests (including business colleagues of the parents) and an average expenditure of $30,000 for the ceremony, reception, and honeymoon. To offset the cost, guests are expected to give the newlyweds gift money, *goshugi,* generally about ¥20,000. To avoid the entire wedding ordeal and to save money, a growing number of Japanese couples are opting to get married abroad. Still, like most major Japanese hotels, banquets play a key role in the Akasaka Prince's economic well being, accounting for as much as 60 percent of its revenue. Restaurants are also a large part of a hotel's mainstay and in the finer hotels offer some of the best cuisine in Tokyo.

Just past the hotel is the Nagatacho subway station; across the busy intersection is Akasaka-Mitsuke station.

Take a Break The Akasaka Prince Hotel has a number of fine dining facilities. At the top of the scale is **Le Trianon,** a French restaurant occupying a stately European-style building built more than 60 years ago as part of the residence of the imperial family and resembling a noble's hunting lodge with wooden cross beams and gleaming chandeliers. It's open daily from noon to 2:30pm and 8 to 10pm. **Blue Gardenia,** on the 40th floor, is the hotel's main dining room, offering superb views of the city and open daily from 11:30am to 2:30pm and 6 to 11pm, while the **Potomac** coffee shop offers quick service and American food daily from 6am to 2am. Other restaurants serve Chinese food, steaks, tempura, and other Japanese cuisine. For a cocktail, however, nothing equals the **Top of Akasaka,** a fancy and romantic lounge on the 40th floor. This is a great perch from which to watch the day fade into darkness, as millions of lights and neon signs twinkle on in the distance. It's open Monday to Saturday from noon to 2am and Sunday from 11:30am to midnight.

There are also unlimited dining and drinking possibilities in Akasaka's nightlife district. One of my favorites on warm summer evenings is the **Suntory Beer Garden,** located atop the Suntory Building. Open June through August Monday to Saturday from 5 to 9pm, it features—what else—Suntory beer, table-top barbecues of sirloin, beef, or ram, and the usual beer snacks. Wonder of wonders, real plants encircle the dining area, and there's not a blade of Astroturf in sight. For more sophisticated (and expensive) Japanese dining, head to **Ten-ichi (天一),** Misuji-dori (tel. 3583-0107), a well-known tempura restaurant open every day except Sunday from 11:30am to 9:30pm, or **Sushi-sei (寿司清),** Misuji-dori (tel. 3586-6446), a moderately priced sushi chain open every day except Sunday from 11:30am to 2:30pm and 5 to 10:30pm. For a unique dining experience, try **Inakaya (田舎家),** 3-12-7 Akasaka (tel. 3586-3054) on Tamachi-dori. Whenever I'm playing hostess to foreign visitors, I always take them here for the drama of it. Customers sit at a long counter, on the other side of which is piled mountains of seafood, beef, and vegetables. In the middle of all that food are two male cooks seated in front of a grill, ready to cook whatever you want. Waiters shout out orders, the cooks shout back, with the result that there is always this excited yelling going on. A lot of fun but expensive, it's open daily from 5 to 11pm. Finally, **Hayashi (はやし),** on the fourth floor at 2-14-1 Akasaka (tel. 3582-4078), is a cozy, rustic-style restaurant specializing in grilled food, which you cook yourself over your own square hibachi. Two set meals are available, with dinner served every day except Sunday from 5:30 to 11pm.

RYOGOKU, ASAKUSABASHI & AKIHABARA— SUMO TOWN, DOLL TOWN & ELECTRIC TOWN

Chuo line to (Tokyo direction)
Ochanomizu.
  ↳ Yellow <u>Sōbu</u> line
    Ryōgoku, Asakusabashi,
Akihabara.
    ↳ Yamanote line .(twd: Ueno, Shibuya,
       etc.)

Start: Edo-Tokyo Museum, 1-4-1 Yokoami. Station: Ryogoku, then the west exit.

Finish: Akihabara Electric Town. Station: Akihabara.

Time: Allow approximately five hours, including stops along the way.

Best Times: Tuesday through Friday, when everything is open.

Worst Times: Monday, when the Edo-Tokyo Museum is closed. Weekends, when the Sumo Museum is closed (note that during sumo tournaments, the museum is open only to those who have tickets to the tournament).

During the Edo Period, craftsmen with the same skills or merchants selling the same merchandise often settled together in the same neighborhood, setting up shop in the front room and living with their families in the back. Thus, merchants selling sweets might live along one street, while craftsmen specializing in bamboo buckets might live along another.

In today's Tokyo there are still traces of such neighborhoods, evident in this stroll. The tour starts in Ryogoku, located on the east side of the Sumida River, which has served as Tokyo's sumo town since the 17th century when wrestling matches were held at a temple here. In addition to a large sumo stadium and a museum dedicated to sumo, Ryogoku also has about a dozen sumo stables, where wrestlers live and train. Easy to spot not only because of their size but also because of their white-and-blue yukata robes and topknot, these giants are often seen roaming the streets of Ryogoku and eating in the district's many restaurants that specialize in chanko nabe, a meal popular with sumo wrestlers for its nutrition and carbohydrates. Ryogogku is also home to one of Tokyo's newer museums, the excellent Edo-Tokyo Museum, which traces the history of the city through the ages. It, together with the Tokyo National Museum in Ueno, ranks as one of the top must-see museums in Tokyo.

Just across the river from Ryogoku is Asakusabashi. In Edo times, it was from here that boats departed for the pleasure quarter of Yoshiwara, giving Asakusabashi a reputation of its own for the many teahouses that lined the river banks and its festive atmosphere. Asakusabashi has also long been the city's wholesale district for dolls. East of Asakusabashi is one of Japan's most famous wholesale districts, Akihabara, with the largest concentration of electronic and electrical shops in Japan.

• • • • • • • • • • • • • • •

Take the Sobu Line to Ryogoku Station and exit from the station's west end, marked by a sign that reads "Kokugikan." On the way out of the station you'll see a large hall and gateway to the right, open only during sumo tournaments and lined with portraits of former grand champions. After exiting the station walk around to the right, following signs that point to the Edo-Tokyo Museum and walking past the sumo stadium (more on that later). Walk up the stairs, to the futuristic-looking:

1. **Edo-Tokyo Museum,** 1-4-1 Yokoami, Sumida-ku (tel. 3626-9974). When viewed from afar, the building is said to resemble a rice granary, but to me it also looks like a modern torii, the entrance gate to a shrine. More than 10 years in the making and opened in 1993, this is the metropolitan government's ambitious attempt to present the history, art, disasters, science, culture, architecture—in other words, everything—of Tokyo from its humble beginnings in 1590, when the first shogun, Ieyasu Tokugawa, came to Edo, to 1964, when Tokyo hosted the Olympics.

After purchasing your admission ticket, take the escalator to the sixth floor, where you'll enter the museum by walking over a replica of Nihombashi Bridge, the starting point for all roads leading out of old Edo. The museum's Edo Zone portrays life in old Edo, the old name for Tokyo and capital of the Tokugawa shogun from 1603 to 1868, with displays relating to the shoguns, merchants, craftsmen, and townspeople. Although explanations are unfortunately mostly in Japanese, there's plenty to look at, from a replica of an old Kabuki theater built in its original size to a model of a luxurious daimyo residence. There are maps showing the layout of old Edo, a collection of woodblock prints with a vivid display on how they're produced, floats used in festivals, and a model of the Mitsui Echigoya dry goods store, the forerunner of Mitsukoshi department store (note how the bolts of material, used for kimono, were kept in a warehouse and were brought out separately to show prospective customers; later, when the store began displaying its wares on shelves in full view of the customers, it was the first store in Japan to do so). Of particular interest is a rowhouse tenement, where Edo commoners lived in cramped quarters measuring only 10 square meters. Note the lack of furniture or closets—futons were simply folded and placed in a corner, while clothing was stored in a bamboo basket. Displays continue in the Tokyo Zone, beginning with the rapid advances made after the Meiji Restoration and continuing through the Great Kanto Earthquake of 1923

Ryogoku, Asakusabashi & Akihabara

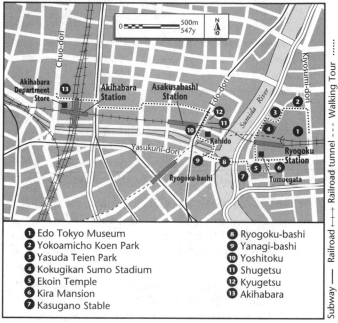

1. Edo Tokyo Museum
2. Yokoamicho Koen Park
3. Yasuda Teien Park
4. Kokugikan Sumo Stadium
5. Ekoin Temple
6. Kira Mansion
7. Kasugano Stable
8. Ryogoku-bashi
9. Yanagi-bashi
10. Yoshitoku
11. Shugetsu
12. Kyugetsu
13. Akihabara

and the bombing raids of World War II up until the 1960s (disappointing is the fact that like most Japanese museums covering the years of World War II, the role of Japan as aggressor is glossed over in favor of Tokyo as a victim of fire bombings in 1944 and 1945). On display are a replica of the *Choya Shimbun* newspaper office, a rickshaw, cameras, bicycles, and a model of the Ginza brick town, the nation's showcase of Western architecture and goods since the Meiji Era. You'll want to spend at least an hour in the museum, open from 10am to 6pm, except on Fridays when it's open from 10am to 9pm and on Mondays when it's closed. You might want to stop by the small first-floor museum shop, which carries books relating to Tokyo, reproductions of old maps, postcards, jewelry with designs inspired by museum pieces, ceramics, porcelains, noren, paper products, toys, T-shirts, and other souvenirs.

Take a Break There are several dining facilities in the **Edo-Tokyo Museum** itself. On the seventh floor is a Japanese restaurant specializing in Edo cuisine, as well as an informal coffeeshop with a view of Tokyo Bay. For Western-style food, try the second-floor Restaurant Moa. A first-floor tea shop features Japanese tea and bean paste sweets. If these restaurants are full, you're in a hurry, or are on a budget, there's an obento lunch-box stall near the main escalator on the same level where you purchased your admission ticket.

Exit the museum in the opposite direction from which you entered (that is, by its east exit), by walking down the stairs and then turning left onto Kiyosumi-dori. After a three-minute walk, to your left will soon be:

2. **Yokoamicho Koen Park,** which now serves as a memorial to those who died in the Great Kanto Earthquake of 1923 and the fire bombings of 1944 and 1945. Upon entering the park, you will soon see a brick building to your right, the Memorial Museum for the Kanto Earthquake Disaster. It serves as a somber reminder of that fateful day on September 1, 1923, when a huge earthquake shook the city at noon. Buildings collapsed, and then a huge fire raged, buffeted by strong winds and fed by homes made of wood. The land you are now standing on was a vacant lot back then, as the Army Clothing Depot had just been relocated to a new location and the 15 acres left empty was in the process of being turned into a public park. Hoping that the empty space might save them from the raging fires, people from throughout the area fled to this vacant lot, but to no avail. Within a few hours this place too was engulfed in flames, suffocating and burning 38,000 people to death. The two-story museum here, free to the public and open every day except Monday from 9am to 4:30pm, contains photographs of the destruction wrought by the disaster, as well as burned personal effects that had belonged to victims. Upstairs the museum holdings have been expanded to cover the destruction of Tokyo during World War II, with more photographs (including one showing Japanese women learning how to use bayonets as defense against American invaders), paintings, and U.S. postwar posters asking for donations to aid the Japanese people.

Near the museum is a temple-like building, topped with a pagoda, the Cenotaph Hall built to commemorate victims of the Great Kanto Earthquake but also serving as a memorial to the more than 100,000 Tokyoites who perished during World War II bombing raids. Large urns hold ashes of earthquake victims, while more photographs and murals depict quake and wartime destruction. If you take a right turn out of the cenotaph, you will see the touching Statue of Unfortunate Children, erected by teachers and classmates in memory of the more than 5,000 children who perished during the Great Kanto Earthquake.

Exit the park by walking around behind the cenotaph, contemplating the fact that Japan has been plagued by earthquakes throughout its existence—indeed, Tokyo has more than 50 earthquakes a year—and that the big one has long been predicted to strike at any time. Catty-corner across the intersection is:

3. **Yasuda Teien Park,** which opened to the public a year after the 1923 earthquake. It was originally constructed during the Edo Period by a daimyo and was considered one of the most beautiful landscaped gardens in the city. Those days now seem long gone, but it remains a pleasant place for a stroll and admission is free.

Since the rear exit of the garden is open only during sumo tournaments, you'll probably have to leave the garden via the same way you entered, turning right out of the park and then heading for the sumo stadium. Follow the road as it curves to the right around the park, and then turn left to reach the main (west) entrance to:

4. **Kokugikan Sumo Stadium,** 1-3-28 Yokoami, built in 1985 and seating 11,500. Japan's national sport, sumo is thought to have originated in Japan more than 1,500 years ago. Of the six Grand Tournaments now held every year, three are held here in this stadium, in January, May, and September, with each tournament lasting 15 consecutive days. Tickets go on sale here at 9am every morning of the tournament, with the first bouts beginning at 10am and the top wrestlers competing from about 4 to 6pm. At the farthest door of the main entrance is the Sumo Museum (tel. 3662-0366), open Monday through Friday from 9:30am to 4:30pm. Admission is free, but note that during tournaments you must be in possession of a sumo ticket to

enter the stadium and therefore the museum. The museum consists mainly of photographs of past and present Grand Champions (called *yokozuna*), the highest rank of sumo wrestlers. Ask for the museum's English pamphlet.

Exit from the stadium and turn left, walking beneath the overhead railroad tracks and continuing straight. This street is lined with small statues of famous sumo wrestlers, complete with hand imprints of grand champions.

Take a Break   A sumo wrestler's weight is legendary, and to achieve it he has to consume huge portions of foods loaded with carbohydrates. The most famous sumo meal is chanko nabe, a stew of meats, seafood, vegetables, mushrooms, and anything else the cook adds, cooked on a grill on the table. One of the best places to try chanko nabe is at **Tomoegata(巴潟)**, 2-17-6 Ryogoku (tel. 3632-5600), located on the last side street to the left as you walk down the street with the sumo statues. Open daily Monday to Saturday from 11:30am to 10pm and Sunday and holidays from noon to 10pm, it was founded in 1976 by a high-ranked sumo wrestler who retired in 1940 and is now run by the wrestler's son. Seating is at either tables or on a tatami floor, and the menu shows pictures of various chanko nabe, available with chicken, beef, or meatballs with miso sauce or seaweed consommé. During lunch time there's an inexpensive chanko nabe teishoku, or set meal. Tempura, kaiseki, and rice casseroles (donburi) are also available.

The street with the sumo statues terminates at a busy street with a traffic light. Opposite the busy street is the wooden gate to:

5. **Ekoin Temple,** with an eclectic mix of memorials and tombs. On the left side of the pathway to the temple is a huge stone, with the Japanese word for "power" written on it. Long ago, so the legend goes, retiring sumo wrestlers used to bury their topknots here. Strangely enough, beside the stone is a black memorial to beloved pets who have died. Grieving owners bring their departed pets' bones and ashes to the temple, leaving behind wooden sticks purchased in their animals' memory. Such a reminder of mortality doesn't seem to bother the large number of cats who roam the grounds of the temple. Actually, Ekoin was originally

dedicated to those who lost their lives in the great fire of 1657. Today it serves as a repository for the remains of unidentified dead people, criminals, and those who die in disasters, which are kept in the tower that dominates the temple's grounds. To the right of the tower is the grave of one of the temple's most illustrious occupants, a robber baron known as the Rat Boy who died in 1831. Like Robin Hood, he captured the hearts of his fellow men by stealing to the rich and giving to the poor. In the past, temple-goers used to chip away at his headstone, in the belief that a stone from his tomb would bring good luck. Because the tombstone had to be replaced so many times, a stone has been placed in front of the tomb for those still wishing to incur luck. To the right of the Rat Boy's tomb is a small area dedicated to stillborn babies, those who died in miscarriage, and, most frequently, aborted babies. The rows of statues here represent Jizo, the guardian deity of children, and some have been dressed in aprons and caps by would-be mothers. The temple also contains a typical Japanese cemetery.

Take a right out of Ekoin and then the first right at the gas station. Walk a minute or so, turning left just before the stoplight, down the street with a sign for Honjo-matsuzakacho Park. Soon, to your left, will be a parking garage common to Japan—a very narrow four-level garage that moves cars in a Ferris-wheel fashion. All car owners in Tokyo must have off-street parking, for which they pay dearly, making car ownership something of a luxury. Just beyond the garage, on the left, is all that remains of:

6. **Kira Mansion,** 3-13-9 Ryogoku. Once a huge estate belonging to Kira, a feudal lord, today it consists only of a white-and-black wall crowned by a weeping willow, and a small inner courtyard. The estate lives on in legend, however, tied to an incident forever immortalized in a Kabuki play. In 1701, Kira was ordered by the Tokugawa shogun to instruct another daimyo, Asano, in the etiquette of court ritual in preparation for a visit from an imperial entourage. The two quarreled, and Asano, quick of temper, drew his sword. Since the drawing of a sword in Edo Castle was strictly forbidden, Asano was ordered to commit ritual

Sumo

Sumo is a Japanese form of wrestling that has been practiced for more than 1,500 years, with the first recorded
match occurring in 200 AD. During the Nara Period, tournaments were staged annually by the imperial court as a
religious ritual to celebrate peace and bountiful harvests,
with wrestlers from all over the country competing. Later,
during the Edo Period, sumo tournaments were often held
to raise funds for the construction of shrines, temples,
and bridges.

Quickly summarized, a sumo match takes place on a
raised, sandy floor, called a dohyo, with the bout itself
confined to a ring about 15 feet in diameter. The object
of the match is for one wrestler to force his opponent out
of the ring or to cause him to touch the ground with any
part of his body other than his feet, even if it's only the
tip of his finger or topknot. This is accomplished by shov-
ing, pushing, slapping, tripping, throwing, and even carrying the opponent. There are as many as 48 sumo holds,
and real fans know them all.

During a 15-day Grand Tournament, each wrestler
(*rikishi*) fights every day with a different opponent, with
the winner of the tournament the wrestler with the most
wins. There are approximately 800 professional rikishi,
but only those of a certain rank are allowed to compete in
a Grand Tournament. Matches begin in the morning
between wrestlers of the lower ranks, followed by those
of progressively higher and higher rank, climaxing at the
end of the day with bouts featuring the yokozuna, or grand
champions. To become a yokozuna, a wrestler must have
attained the rank of *ozeki,* which is the next-highest
rank to a yokozuna, and must be the winner of two
consecutive Grand Tournaments. Once the rikishi becomes a yokozuna, he can never be demoted, even if he
subsequently performs poorly, but if he continues with a

suicide, his family was disinherited and turned out of
its home, his estate and castle were confiscated by the
shogun, and his retainers became *ronin,* masterless

bad record he is expected to retire. Since the title of yokozuna was created more than 300 years ago, fewer than 65 rikishi have ever attained the rank of yokozuna. They are idolized by Japanese sumo fans, similar to basketball or baseball stars in the west.

Because of its historical ties to Shintoism, a sumo tournament abounds in ceremonies and practices dating from the Edo Period and beyond. During opening ceremonies, held every day of the tournament, the rikishi enter the dohyo with brightly colored aprons. The yokozuna perform the most honored part of the highly stylized ritual, first clapping their hands to attract the attention of the gods and then extending their arms to their sides with palms upward, to prove they are concealing no weapons. They then lift first one leg high into the air and then the other, stamping them on the ground to crush any evil spirits that might be lurking there.

At the beginning of each match, the two rikishi symbolically cleanse their mind and body by rinsing their mouths with water, just as worshippers rinse their mouths before visiting a Shinto shrine. They then stamp their feet, show their palms to prove they aren't carrying any weapons, and scatter salt in the ring to purify it. The two wrestlers then squat and face each other, their fists on the ground, and glare fiercely at each other in a staring match. Rarely do they begin the match at this point, but rather begin a short period of cold psychological warfare, standing up and going back to their corners to scatter more salt and glaring at each other again. There's a four-minute time limit imposed on the higher ranks for the standoff, with lower ranks having only three minutes and the lowest ranks having to begin their bout right away. At any rate, this starting and stopping again creates excitement in both the wrestlers and the fans. Once the rikishi lunge toward each other, the match is usually over in a matter of minutes and sometimes even seconds.

samurai. Kira, on the other hand, went unpunished, which drew widespread criticism since it was generally the custom to punish both sides in a fight. Forty-seven ronin decided to avenge their master's death by killing Kira, which they did here at this mansion. There's a well in the corner of the small courtyard here where the ronin were said to have washed Kira's severed head, which they then paraded through the streets of Edo on the way to their master's grave. The public was captivated by their loyalty to their dead master, but the shogun ordered all of them to commit ritual suicide through disembowelment. A stone outside the Kira mansion commemorates the 47 ronin.

Take a right out of the Kira courtyard and retrace your steps, this time continuing straight and passing more parking garages. Turn left at the busy street and then take the first immediate right. To your right is:

7. **Kasugano Stable,** 1-7-11 Ryogoku, one of the most well-known and prosperous sumo stables (called *heya*) in Ryogoku. An imposing modern building with such traditional flourishes as a shrine-like roof over the entryway and a bamboo fence, it's the domain of sumo wrestlers, most of whom live and also train here. Apprentices usually begin their training at about age 15, reaching their peak in their 20s and retiring in their early 30s. Incidentally, it's not unusual nowadays to see sumo wrestlers from Hawaii and Micronesia. Akebono, from Hawaii, was the first foreigner to achieve the rank of yokozuna, in 1993. On the right side of the Kasugano Stable is a door—if it's open, you might be able to peek inside for a look at the practicing arena, where you'll see wrestlers practicing or, if it's during their break, sleeping.

From the stable, return to the busy street and turn left, walk to the street light and then turn left again. Soon you will come to:

8. **Ryogokubashi.** The bridge was first built after the huge 1657 fire, when thousands of people died at the banks of the bridgeless Sumida river, trying to escape the flames. Its name means "Bridge of the Two Provinces," and during the Edo Period a kind of carnival atmosphere prevailed at its eastern end, complete with jugglers, acrobats, exotic animals, and other forms of entertainment. An annual fireworks display added to the Sumida's popularity, and in summer, pleasure boats drifted along the river. As you cross the bridge, note the banks of the river—unlike most of the

Sumida, the banks here have recently been turned into a much-needed urban park.

After crossing the bridge, turn right at the second stoplight, just before the Shell gas station, for:

9. **Yanagibashi,** a picturesque small bridge adorned, interestingly enough, with hairpins women once wore in their hair. Yanagibashi means "Willow Tree Bridge," and there are still willow trees here, but it's most remembered as the starting point for boats heading for Yoshiwara, Edo's licensed pleasure quarter. Some pleasure seekers never made it farther than Yanagibashi, however, which developed a small but flourishing unlicensed pleasure quarter of its own. During the warm summer months, geisha boats plied the waters of the nearby Sumida. A hint of that remains, with gaily decorated dining boats now moored on the canal beneath the bridge and available for group parties.

Turn left after crossing Yanagibashi. There's a tiny shop here, beside the bridge and willow tree, called Komatsuya, which has been selling tskudani, tiny dried fish, for more than 50 years. Take a peek inside, and then walk alongside the canal to the next, and turn right. This is Edo-dori, Tokyo's wholesale district for dolls. On your left side will soon be:

10. **Yoshitoku,** 1-9-14 Asakusabashi (tel. 3863-4419), Tokyo's oldest wholesale doll and traditional crafts store. A purveyor to the Imperial household and established in 1711, it sells a variety of Japanese dolls on its first floor, most traditionally dressed as samurai, geisha, Kabuki actors, sumo wrestlers, and other Japanese personalities. There are also fine—and expensive—dolls representing the imperial court, dressed in silk kimono that follow the originals down to the minutest detail. These dolls are not for play but for display, and there's even a special day set aside for the occasion, called Hinamatsuri, or Doll Festival, celebrated as Girl's Day on March 3. That's when girls throughout Japan set up their collection of dolls, which numbers 15 when complete and consists of an emperor and empress and members of the royal court. Some dolls are passed down from generation to generation as heirlooms, and the collection often contains doll-size miniatures, such as palanquins. If you're in Japan during this festival, you'll probably find

collections of dolls also on display at major hotels. At any rate, upstairs are mundane dolls, including modern stuffed animals and even Mickey Mouse. It's open Monday to Saturday from 9:30am to 5:30pm.

Continue walking north, where just past the overhead tracks to the right is the brown building of:

11. **Shugetsu (秀月),** 1-20-3 Yanagibashi (tel. 3861-8801), open daily from 10am to 6pm. It displays dolls on its ground floor, while the second floor is devoted to the sale of kimono and kimono accessories. Almost next door is:

12. **Kyugetsu,** 1-20-4 Yanagibashi (tel. 5687-5176), founded in 1830 and one of the area's biggest doll shops. Open Monday through Friday from 9:15am to 6pm, it sells both traditional and modern dolls, as well as stuffed animals, on two floors.

Take a Break   On the south side of the overhead tracks, to the east of Edo-dori, is an unremarkable building on a corner, with an interior that comes as a total surprise with its heavy wood beams, wooden floor, and jazz playing softly in the background. Called **Kahido (我楽),** 1-14-3 Yanagibashi (tel. 3851-4538), it has a family of badger statues beckoning at its entrance and a display of lovely tea and coffee cups lining the wall behind the counter. It's a relaxing place for a cup of coffee, tea, coffee float, or iced coffee and is open Monday to Friday from 9am to 10pm, Saturday from 9am to 7pm and Sunday from noon to 7pm.

If you're ready to call it quits, the overhead tracks at Edo-dori is Asakusabashi Station, serviced by the Sobu Line. Nearby is the underground station of the same name, where you can board the Toei Asakusa train.

If, however, you're interested in seeing the largest electrical and electronics district in Japan, you can walk due west, along the road that runs beside the overhead train tracks, arriving after 10 minutes or so in:

13. **Akihabara** (you can also reach Akihabara by taking the Sobu Line one stop; exit Akihabara Station via the Chuo-dori/Akihabara Electric Town exit). If you're walking, you must walk around Akihabara Station and under the tracks to reach Denki Electric Town. At any rate, with

more than 600 stores, shops, and stalls, most centered along Chuo-dori, Akihabara accounts for one-tenth of the nation's electronic and electrical appliance sales. Even if you don't buy anything, it's great fun walking around, looking at the latest in electronic gadgetry long before it hits western shores. Most of the stores and stalls are open-fronted, with lights flashing, TVs blaring, fans whirring, washing machines shaking, and hawkers trying to sell refrigerators, rice cookers, watches, pocket calculators, stereos, cassette and CD players, camcorders, fax machines, computers, and more. If you do plan on buying something, make sure it's made for export—that is, that there are instructions in English, that there is an international warranty, and that the product has the correct electrical connectors. Be sure, too, to comparison shop; all the larger shops have tax-free floors where the products are especially designed for export. Most shops are open daily from 10am to 7pm. The nearest station here, of course, is Akihabara.

Take a Break   **Akihabara Department Store,** located at the west end of Akihabara Station, has a fast-food department on its ground floor. Individual counters, with sit-down service, offer curry dishes, Edo-style sushi, okonomiyaki (Japanese-style pancakes), donburi-mono (rice casseroles), hamburgers, noodles, and coffee. Simply walk around and decide what looks best. It's open daily from 10:30am to 7pm.

Shibuya—
Fashion Town

Start: Hachiko Square. Station: Shibuya.

Finish: Shibuya Center Gai. Station: Shibuya.

Time: Allow approximately two hours for the walk itself, not including shopping, sightseeing, or breaks along the way.

Best Times: Most times of the day and week are fine for this tour.

Worst Times: Monday, when the Tobacco & Salt Museum is closed. Wednesday, when the Tepco Electric Energy Museum and stores belonging to the Seibu chain are closed.

It would be hard to rhapsodize about Shibuya, and yet most Tokyoites have a soft spot in their hearts for this personable neighborhood, if for no other reason than because of a dog. Shibuya is known throughout Japan as the home of Hachiko, an Akita that lived more than a half century ago but is still remembered for its steadfast loyalty to its master. Located on the southwestern edge of the Yamanote loop line, Shibuya grew in the 1920s as a thriving suburb, especially after the 1923 earthquake which destroyed much of the inner city, causing many businesses to relocate to the virtually untouched western part of the capital.

With the suburbs now reaching far beyond, Shibuya serves as an important commuter nucleus, with two subway lines and four railway lines converging at Shibuya Station. To tap in to the 700,000 or so passengers who pass through the station daily, nightlife and shopping have emerged as Shibuya's main draws. Catering primarily to students and young office workers, Shibuya is more subdued than Shinjuku, more down to earth than Harajuku, and certainly less cosmopolitan than Roppongi. By day, Shibuya is a shopper's paradise for fashion and interior decorations, with the greatest concentration of specialty department stores in the city. Tokyu and Seibu are the two big names here, both of which have opened so many branches in Shibuya that a bona fide store war has been raging for more than a decade. When night falls, the action centers on a pedestrian street just a stone's throw from the station, which offers commuters a wide choice of inexpensive yakitori-ya, bars, noodle shops, pachinko parlors, and fast-food restaurants. Add to that a couple of unique museums, and Shibuya makes for an interesting day's outing, especially if, like me, you enjoy browsing around stores, just to see what's there.

● ● ● ● ● ● ● ● ● ● ● ● ● ● ● ●

No matter which line you take to Shibuya Station, look for signs directing you to:

1. **Hachiko Square.** This outdoor plaza, located on the north end of the station, serves as Shibuya's most well-known meeting place and is usually packed with young Japanese waiting for friends, dates, and business acquaintances. The square's namesake was once a common sight at the station, waiting patiently for his master, a university professor, to return home every day from work. When the professor died in the mid-1920s, Hachiko continued to come to the station every day for the next decade, waiting faithfully for a master who never returned. The dog's death made the national news, prompting donations to pour in from throughout the country for the erection of a statue in his honor. You'll find Hachiko's statue at one end of the square, underneath the trees, barely visible through the crowds of

people who have arranged beforehand to "meet at Hachiko." The stuffed hide of Hachiko, by the way, is on view at the National Science Museum in Ueno.

With your back to the station and facing the plethora of signs ahead, walk towards the building with the big Sony screen. This is:

2. **109-2,** 1-23-10 Jinnan (tel. 3477-8111), one of several One-Oh-Nine fashion stores in Shibuya. Appealing to office workers in their 20s, this fashion store offers seven floors of boutiques carrying lines that are largely unknown outside Japan, including clothing and accessories ranging from belts and shoes to handbags, umbrellas, and cosmetics. It's open daily from 10am to 9pm.

Across the street on the left side is:

3. **Seibu,** 21-1 Udagawacho (tel. 3462-0111), one of Shibuya's largest department stores and consisting of two buildings connected by pedestrian skywalks. Seibu A contains women's fashions, including many designer labels such as Valentino, Calvin Klein, Missoni, Sonia Rykiel, Comme des Garcons, Yohji Yamamoto, Krizia, and Donna Karan. Seibu B carries men's fashion, children's clothing, an art gallery, and interior decorations and furniture. Both are open from 10am to 7pm, closed on Wednesday.

Take the road that runs between Seibu A and B. At the first right is:

4. **Loft,** 21-1 Udagawacho (tel. 3462-0111), Seibu's store for the homeowner and hobbyist, with an eye toward the trendy. It's crowded with young shoppers in search of simple furniture, games, telephones, stationery, office supplies, cookware, glassware, and more. On the sixth floor is a "designer's corner," with well-designed products from various countries. Displays change often but may include ashtrays, clocks, paperweights, boxes, jewelry, vases, desk-top items, and other interesting gifts and knickknacks. Loft is open from 11am to 8pm, closed on the second and third Wednesday of every month.

From the first floor of Loft, walk through the adjoining Wave, which sells music cassettes and compact discs, and then turn left for:

Shibuya—Fashion Town

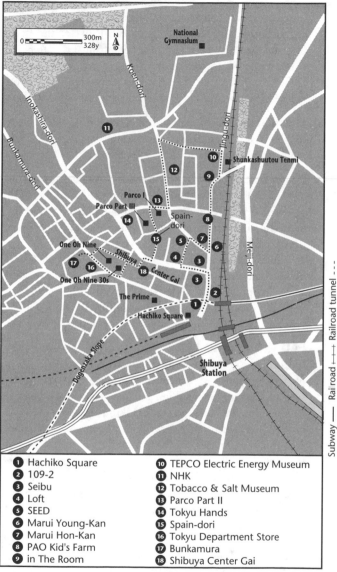

1. Hachiko Square
2. 109-2
3. Seibu
4. Loft
5. SEED
6. Marui Young-Kan
7. Marui Hon-Kan
8. PAO Kid's Farm
9. in The Room
10. TEPCO Electric Energy Museum
11. NHK
12. Tobacco & Salt Museum
13. Parco Part II
14. Tokyu Hands
15. Spain-dori
16. Tokyu Department Store
17. Bunkamura
18. Shibuya Center Gai

5. **SEED,** 21-1 Udagawacho (tel. 3462-0111), Seibu's fashion department store. It offers eight floors of the newest of the new, but because each story is fairly small it won't take you as long as you might think to work your way through the various boutiques, where you'll find a lot of names you may

or may not be familiar with, along with such well-knowns as Paul Smith, Katharine Hamnett, Jean-Paul Gaultier, Betsy Johnson, and Osamu Maeda. It's open from 11am to 8pm, closed some Wednesdays.

Take a right out of SEED and walk downhill, where you will see:

6. **Marui Young-Kan,** 1-22-6 Jinnan (tel. 3464-0101). Look for the chain's logo, 0101. This branch, together with the main store across the street:

7. **Marui Hon-Kan,** 1-23-3 Jinnan (tel. 3464-0101), is geared toward young people, especially those who are new to the work force and are buying clothes and items for their apartments for the first time. Many young Japanese get their first credit cards here. The main shop has clothing and accessories as well as furniture and kitchenware, while Marui Young-Kan carries mainly fashion. Both stores are open from 11am to 8pm, closed some Wednesdays.

Walking north on the road that separates Marui Young-Kan and Hon-Kan, Jingu-dori, to your right will soon be:

8. **PAO Kid's Farm,** 1-22-14 Jinnan (tel. 5458-0111), the ultimate in a children's department store. It has eight floors of everything imaginable, much of it imported (and expensive) and ranging from fashion and games to dolls and books. If you're looking for that perfect Ralph Lauren or Kenzo outfit for junior or chopsticks with Sesame Street characters, this is the place. Very user-friendly, the store even has free rental strollers, video and amusement game corners, a play area for toddlers, a rooftop playground, diaper-changing areas, cots for naps, and restrooms designed with kids in mind. It's open from 10:30am to 6:30pm, closed most Wednesdays.

Take a Break   In the basement of PAO Kid's Farm is **Anna Miller's** (tel. 5458-4108), a U.S. chain of family-style restaurants that has taken Tokyo by storm. Famous for its pies, with about a hundred varieties to tempt you, it offers American food ranging from spaghetti and fried shrimp to hamburger steak, as well as lunch specials and kids' meals. It's open from 10:30am to 10pm daily. Down the street, across from in The Room and TEPCO (see below), is **Shunkashuutou Tenmi,** 1-10-6 Jinnan (tel. 3496-9703), located on the second floor above Pure Food Square, a health-food store. This reasonably priced restaurant specializes in Japanese macrobiotic vegetarian meals, including various vegetable, tofu, buckwheat noodle, and brown rice combinations. It's open weekdays from 11:30am to 2pm and 5 to 9pm, Saturday from 11:30am to 7pm and Sunday from 11:30am to 6pm. It's closed the second and third Wednesday of every month.

From PAO Kid's Farm and continuing north, in the next block on the left is:

9. **in The Room,** 1-12-13 Jinnan (tel. 3464-0101), Marui's answer to Seibu's Loft and offering six floors of home furnishings and decorations, including everything you need for the living room, dining room, bathroom, bedroom, and kitchen. It's open from 11am to 8pm, closed some Wednesdays.

Next door is the:

10. **TEPCO Electric Energy Museum,** 1-12-10 Jinnan (tel. 3477-1191), a public-service facility of the Tokyo Electric Power Company (TEPCO), which operates 14 nuclear power plants that supply Tokyo and its vicinity with electricity. Established to teach urban dwellers how electricity is generated, supplied, and consumed, it offers five floors of displays, including a model of a nuclear reactor, a "house of the future" equipped with the latest in appliances and technology, and a play area geared toward children with computers and games. The museum, free to the public, is spotless and well designed, and with machines humming, lights blinking, and polite, uniformed women with pillbox hats standing at attention to answer every question, you're excused for thinking you've somehow landed on the starship *Enterprise.* It's open every except Wednesday from 10:30am to 6:30pm.

Take a left out of the TEPCO museum and then another immediate left, just before the fire station. Walk straight uphill a couple of minutes until the road ends at a big street, Koen-dori. To your right you'll see the National Gymnasium, built for the 1964 Olympics, and the headquarters of:

11. **NHK,** which stands for Nihon Hoso Kyokai, or Japan Broadcasting Corporation. Facilities here consist of a 23-story glass office building and a smaller building housing more than 20 TV studios, as well as radio studios, recording studios, and an auditorium that seats 4,000. More than 1,500 TV and radio programs are produced here weekly for national broadcast. If you want, you can enter the free visitor's center and follow a short do-it-yourself 2,000-foot walking tour that will take you past some studios and panel displays depicting some of NHK's most successful past programs, but explanations are in Japanese only and opening hours are irregular.

    Turn left onto Koen-dori and walk downhill. You will soon see a brick building on your left, the:

12. **Tobacco & Salt Museum,** 1-16-8 Jinnan (tel. 3476-2041). It seems strange to combine both commodities in one museum, especially considering how unpopular both tobacco and salt have become in today's health-conscious world. However, both were once ruled by a government monopoly and are therefore featured together here, with displays that relate the history of Japanese and foreign salt and tobacco, packaging from throughout the world, woodblock prints that show people smoking, and special changing exhibitions. It's open every day except Monday from 10am to 6pm (you must enter by 5:30pm), and a modest admission fee is charged.

    Take a left out of the museum and continue walking downhill, past the shop selling western cowboy boots (!) and a Mister Donut, to the first big, busy intersection where you'll find:

13. **Parco Part II,** 15-1 Udagawacho (tel. 3464-5111), on your right. Just beyond it is Parco Part I. A division of Seibu, Parco is divided into four buildings, called Parco Part I (the main store), Parco Part II, Parco Part III, and Quattro. Parco I and II are fashion department stores filled with designer boutiques for men and women, including such well-known designers and designs as Issey Miyake, Takeo Kikuchi, Comme des Garçons (designer Rei Kawakubo), Yoshiyuki Konishi, and Nicole (designer Mitsuhiro Matsuda), as well as boutiques selling kimono. Parco I has some good

restaurants on its seventh floor. Parco III has more fashions, but its emphasis is on household goods and interiors, and Quattro is for music and videos, with a music venue on its top floor. All are open daily from 10am to 8:30pm.

Take a Break The seventh floor of **Parco Part I** has a number of restaurants specializing in Italian cuisine, Chinese food, sushi, shabu-shabu, kushikatsu (skewered meats and vegetables), tonkatsu (fried pork cutlets), and other Japanese food. Restaurants are open daily from 11am to 11pm.

If you take the road that runs between Parco I and II west in the direction of the Education Center, you will soon come to :

14. **Tokyu Hands,** 12-18 Udagawacho (tel. 5489-5111) on your left. Billing itself as the "Creative Life Store," Tokyu Hands is a huge department store for the homeowner and hobbyist, with departments devoted to camping and picnic equipment, games, gadgets, party supplies, sewing machines, cookware, Japanese knives, plastic lunchboxes, Japanese papers (including shoji paper for those inevitable repairs), office supplies, batteries, travel accessories, knockdown furniture, toiletries, clocks and watches, garden tools, and all the equipment and materials for do-it-yourselfers. If you're setting up an apartment in Tokyo, this is the place to come. It's open from 10am to 8pm, closed the second and third Monday of every month.

Retrace your steps in the direction of Parco, turning right on the second side street just before Parco. After passing the small studio of a Tokyo FM radio station with a large plate-glass window so passersby can stop to watch the live broadcasts, you will find yourself on:

15. **Spain-dori,** a narrow pedestrian shopping lane filled with young people and lined with shops and restaurants catering to youthful tastes. Head down the stairs of Spain-dori, which brings you to a street with cars, Inokashira-dori. Cross it and continue walking straight. The next street you come to, marked by a McDonald's, is Shibuya Center Gai, Shibuya's main nightlife drag (see below). If you've had enough shopping for the day, you might want to call it quits

and have a drink or meal here. If you follow Center Gai to the end (that is, turning left when you reach Center Gai from Spain-dori), you'll find yourself back at Shibuya Station.

Otherwise, if you're game for one more department store giant, don't turn onto Shibuya Center Gai but rather continue walking straight one block and then turn right onto Bunkamura-dori. To your right you'll pass another One-Oh-Nine, open daily from 10am to 9pm and offering clothing, accessories, household goods, a CD shop, and a Body Shop. Next on the right is One-Oh-Nine 30s, which, as its name suggests, tries to draw in slightly older and more sophisticated shoppers in their 30s with its smart, upscale boutiques.

Across the way is:

16. **Tokyu department store,** 2-24-1 Dogenzaka (tel. 3477-3111), the other big name in Shibuya. This is the main store of this huge chain, which appeals mainly to a 30s and up group with its conservative styles in clothing and housewares. You'll find women's clothes on the third and fourth floors, men's fashions on the second floor, children's clothing and toys on the seventh floor, and arts and crafts and restaurants on the eighth floor. It's open every day except Tuesday from 10am to 7pm.

Adjacent to Tokyu is the company's ultramodern:

17. **Bunkamura entertainment complex** (tel. 3477-9111), which features a concert and performance hall with such diverse programs as ballet, philharmonic orchestras, and concerts; two cinemas (the Tokyo Film Festival is held here); a theater; a museum with changing exhibitions of mainly modern art; an art gallery; and shops and cafés. Bunkamura's name means "culture village."

From Tokyu, retrace your steps back on Bunkamura-dori, which leads to Shibuya Station. I suggest, however, that you return to Shibuya Station via:

18. **Shibuya Center Gai,** which you can reach by turning left after Nine-Oh-Nine 30s and then right onto Center Gai, a pedestrian lane colorful with neon signs and blinking lights advertising inexpensive restaurants, bars, fast-food

joints, and pachinko parlors. Catering to young office workers and students, these establishments are pretty straight-
forward and reasonably priced—you'll even find KFC,
Arby's, and McDonald's here.

Take a Break   Restaurants on the eighth floor of
Tokyu department store, open until 10:30pm,
offer Chinese, French, Italian, and Japanese food. On the
fourth floor of **Tokyu** is Laura Ashley, an English-style tea
shop featuring waitresses dressed in Laura Ashley pinafores
and Laura Ashley tablecloths and china and offering tea,
coffee, scones, cakes, muffins, sandwiches, and apple pie.
It's open every day except Tuesday from 10am to 7pm.
Shibuya Center Gai, Shibuya's main nightlife street, is lined
with restaurants and bars offering everything from noodles
and hamburgers to sushi and yakitori. Otherwise, one of
my favorite places for an inexpensive and easy meal in
Shibuya is in **The Prime,** 2-29-5 Dogenzaka (tel. 3770-
0111), located on Dogenzaka Slope and part of the Seibu
conglomerate. An entertainment complex with movie
theaters, a dance and aerobics studio, and a concert and
theater ticket agency, it has a great second-floor cafeteria,
with various counters offering dishes from around the world,
including Indian curries, Chinese food, pasta, sandwiches,
bagels, salads, sushi, noodles, desserts, and drinks. Simply
walk around and choose what looks good. It's open daily
from 11:30am to 10pm. In the basement of The Prime
are a number of noodle shops serving more types of noodles
than you probably ever dreamed posssible—Chinese,
Singaporean, and Japanese noodles from Kyushu to
Hokkaido, and even spaghetti. The shops here are open
daily from 11am to 11pm.

IKEBUKURO–COMMUTER TOWN

Start: Tobu Department Store, 1-1-25 Nishi-Ikebukuro. Station: Ikebukuro, and then the west exit.

Finish: Ancient Orient Museum, Sunshine City. Station: Ikebukuro or Higashi-Ikebukuro.

Time: The walk itself takes only an hour, but you should allow at least three or four hours to see the sights along the way.

Best Times: If you wish to visit every recommendation in this tour, go on a Friday, Saturday, or Sunday when everything is open. To avoid weekend crowds, go on a Friday.

Worst Times: Monday through Thursday, when some of the department stores and museums are closed.

If it weren't for Seibu and Tobu department stores, Sunshine City, and a handful of specialty shops, few tourists would ever venture to Ikebukuro, located on the northwestern edge of the Yamanote loop line. With its huge station, Ikebukuro has long been a commuter's town, a convenient stopover for those on their way home to Saitama

Prefecture. Geared toward those who live in the boonies, Ikebukuro has always been slighted as the working-man's Tokyo, unsophisticated, crass, and a bit rough around the edges. Part of Ikebukuro's reputation stems from its past—it was the site of the notoriously squalid Sugamo Prison.

But Ikebukuro has changed remarkably in the past decade, and only those who haven't been here the past few years could continue to dismiss it as nothing more than a provincial outpost. Ikebukuro's transformation began with the 1978 completion of Sunshine City, a sprawling complex boasting Japan's tallest building at the time, a first-rate hotel, a huge shopping mall, and attractions ranging from an aquarium and a museum to an observation platform. Seibu built what was once the country's largest department store here, an honor that now goes to nearby rival Tobu. The formerly seedy west side of the station has given rise to the Tokyo Metropolitan Art Space, a graceful structure of glass and steel and a venue for dance, music, and theater. Add to that an indoor antique flea market and a huge ultra-modern Toyota showroom, and Ikebukuro makes for a pleasant half-day's outing even for people who aren't merely passing through.

Of course, Ikebukuro still bustles with commuters, as office workers stop for a quick meal or a couple of drinks and housewives from the outlying suburbs shop at Seibu or Tobu, picking up tonight's dinner from the department stores' massive food floors. But you'll also find families here on Sunday outings, concertgoers, and youthful shoppers, as well as an increasing number of urban sophisticates who look upon Ikebukuro as their own private unstomped grounds. I can't begin to count the number of friends who ten years ago wouldn't be caught dead here, now whispering with a secretive air, "There's this great little place in Ikebukuro . . ."

• • • • • • • • • • • • • • • •

Ikebukuro Station may well earn the distinction of being the most confusing and frustrating in Tokyo. Serving the Marunouchi and Yurakucho subway lines, the Seibu Ikebukuro Line, Tobu Tojo Line, and the Yamanote Line, it has few signs in English. No matter how you arrive, take the west exit and look for signs for:

1. **Tobu department store,** 1-1-25 Nishi-Ikebukuro (tel. 3981-2211), which rises practically above the station and consists of a main building, a connecting central building and Metropolitan Plaza. Once overshadowed by nearby Seibu, this flagship of the Tobu chain reopened in 1993 as Japan's largest department store, employing 3,000 clerks to serve the 180,000 customers who enter its doors daily. Stop by the information booth on the first floor for an English pamphlet of the various departments. Offering everything from luxury goods and the latest international fashions to hardware, software, toys, and daily necessities, it also stocks traditional Japanese products, good for souvenirs. Its basement food floor is massive, reflective of the fact that food accounts for nearly 20 percent of Tobu's total sales. Be sure to check out the:

2. **Tobu Museum of Art** (tel. 5391-3220), located in the Tobu Metropolitan Plaza building. Featuring a broad range of international art, with no restrictions as to genre, period or region, it stages six diverse exhibitions yearly, with past shows centering on Renaissance paintings from the Budapest Museum of Fine Arts, ukiyo-e, works of Japanese artist Yokoyama Taikan, and art from Russia, India, and Australia. Admission is charged, and it's open the same hours as Tobu department store, from 10am to 7pm, closed on Wednesday.

Take a Break If you're indecisive about what to eat, head for the 11th through 17th floors of the **Tobu** main building, which boasts outlets for various famous restaurants serving Japanese, Chinese, and Western cuisine. Known collectively as "Spice," the restaurants here range from okonomiyaki (Japanese-style pancakes/pizza), shabu-shabu, kamameshi (rice casseroles), Japanese steak, and Kyoto-style food to Thai, French, Chinese, and Italian cuisine. More than 20 additional establishments are in the **Metropolitan Plaza's** Restaurant World on the 7th and 8th floors, offering cuisine from around the world and Japanese food such as tonkatsu (breaded pork), tempura, sushi, and noodles. All restaurants are open daily from 11am to 11pm (last order is at 10pm). From May to the end of September, Tobu also has an outdoor beer garden, open from

Ikebukuro—Commuter Town

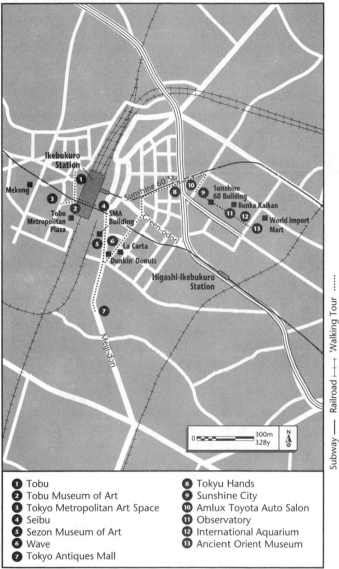

Subway — Railroad ┼┼┼ Walking Tour ⋯⋯

0 ▪▬▬▬▬ 300m
328y

Ikebukuro Station

Mekong

Tobu Metropolitan Plaza

SMA Building

Sunshine 60 St.

Green-odori

Sunshine 60 Building

Bunka Kaikan

World Import Mart

La Carta

Dunkin' Donuts

Higashi-Ikebukuro Station

Meiji-dori

① Tobu
② Tobu Museum of Art
③ Tokyo Metropolitan Art Space
④ Seibu
⑤ Sezon Museum of Art
⑥ Wave
⑦ Tokyo Antiques Mall
⑧ Tokyu Hands
⑨ Sunshine City
⑩ Amlux Toyota Auto Salon
⑪ Observatory
⑫ International Aquarium
⑬ Ancient Orient Museum

9707

5 to 9pm. If Thai food is your love, don't miss **Mekong,** 3-26-5 Nishi-Ikebukuro (tel. 3988-5688), located on the west side of Ikebukuro Station behind the Tokyo Metropolitan Art Space, in a basement under McDonald's. Open daily from 11:30am to 2:30pm and 5 to 11pm, this small

and unpretentious eatery serves dependably good and expertly spiced Thai specialties, at very reasonable prices.

On the west side of Ikebukuro Station, on the other side of the square and fountain, is the modern:

3. **Tokyo Metropolitan Art Space** (tel. 5391-2111), which opened in 1990 as a cultural center for the performing arts. To shield its three auditoriums from outside noise, a three-story waterfall cascades down a 92-foot-high atrium, and facilities include a 1,887-seat concert hall and an 850-seat theater. Call for current listings or visit the ticket counter in the lobby.

From the west side of Ikebukuro Station, take either the central or south underground passage to the station's east side, where you'll find the other department store giant:

4. **Seibu,** 1-28-1 Minami Ikebukuro (tel. 3981-0111). Once the largest department store in the land, it's still mighty impressive, with 47 entrances, 12 floors, and dozens of restaurants. On an average weekday 170,000 shoppers pass through the store. Located practically on top of Ikebukuro Station, it devotes two floors to foodstuffs alone, with dishes set out so you can nibble and sample food as you move along. The other floors feature clothing, furniture, art galleries, kitchenware, and a thousand other things, and many of the best Japanese and Western designers have boutiques here. The top four floors are devoted to interior design, in a section of the store called the Loft. The eighth floor has more than a dozen restaurants offering everything from teppanyaki and sushi to Indian and French cuisine. Seibu is open every day except Tuesday from 10am to 8pm.

Exit Seibu and turn right onto Meiji-dori, where next door to Seibu you'll find the SMA Building, which belongs to the Seibu chain and contains the:

5. **Sezon Museum of Art** (tel. 5992-8700), open every day except Tuesday from 10am to 8pm and charging admission. It specializes in changing exhibitions of Japanese and foreign modern art, with past shows featuring works by Bruno Taut and Klee.

Across the street from SMA is:

6. **Wave** (tel. 5992-0600), a branch of the much larger Roppongi Wave, Japan's first music and film specialty store. Also owned by Seibu, Wave offers a comprehensive range of music, with audio stations with headphones available so patrons can listen to the latest releases. Although the Ikebukuro branch isn't as large as the main store, it's good nonetheless for CD releases of classics and oldies and new recordings of independent labels. It's open every day except Tuesday from 10am to 8pm.

   Turn left out of Wave and continue south on Meiji-dori. After a five-minute walk, you'll arrive at the:

7. **Tokyo Antiques Hall** (Komingu Kottokan), 3-9-5 Minami Ikebukuro (tel. 3982-3433), on the left side of the street. Outdoor flea markets, such as the one held at Togo Shrine in Harajuku, are the best places to look for antiques and collectibles, but because they generally are open only a couple weekends a month, this antique hall is the next best thing. Open Friday to Wednesday from 11am to 7pm (but get there before 5pm, since some stalls close early if business is slow), this antique hall houses more than 35 stalls, owned by dealers who comb flea markets across the country for the best buys. You could spend hours here, looking over furniture, scrolls and screens, calligraphy, hair ornaments, watches, samurai outfits, jewelry, lacquerware, swords, china, Japanese army memorabilia, kimono and fabrics, dolls, and other items too numerous to list. Prices are high, but it doesn't hurt to try to bargain.

   Take a right out of the antiques hall and head back north on Meiji-dori. When you come to the first big intersection, the one with a Dunkin' Donuts on the corner, instead of heading back to SMA and Seibu on Meiji-dori, take the road along the right side of the doughnut shop.

   ☕ Take a Break Just past Dunkin' Donuts, on the right side of the street, is a convenient and easy place for a snack or meal, **La Carta,** 2-16-8 Minami Ikebukuro (tel. 3981-0141), which bills itself as a "Grazing Terrace." Self-serve counters offer various foods, including pasta, pizza, yakitori, snacks, desserts, and drinks. Simply walk around, pick out what you want, and pay when you leave. A good place for just a drink if that's all you want, it's open daily from 11am to 11pm.

About a two-minute walk past Dunkin' Donuts is a busy intersection with a tree-lined street, called Green-Odori. Cross it, and just beyond you'll come to a pedestrian lane, called Sunshine 60 Street, lined with shops and restaurants. Turn right here, following the sign that points to the Sunshine 60 Building. At the end of this street, on the right, is:

8. **Tokyu Hands,** 1-28-10 Higashi-Ikebukuro (tel. 3980-6111), open from 10am to 8pm and closed the second and third Thursdays of each month. A carbon copy of the Tokyu Hands in Shibuya, it stocks everything for the home owner and hobbyist, including hardware, sporting goods, kitchenware, noren, lighting fixtures, drawing supplies, post cards and greeting cards, games, travel supplies, travel bags, and more. Stop by the information book on the ground floor for a pamphlet and store map in English.

At the entrance to Tokyu Hands you'll also find the entryway to:

9. **Sunshine City.** Take the escalator down, and then continue along the moving sidewalk. Sunshine City, built in 1978, consists of three interconnected buildings: the Sunshine 60 Building, a 60-story skyscraper topped by an observation platform and once the tallest building in Japan; the 11-story World Import Mart with a shopping mall, aquarium and planetarium; and the Bunka Kaikan, a cultural center with a museum of ancient artifacts. First, however, I suggest you make a detour to the adjoining:

10. **Amlux Toyota Auto Salon,** 3-3-5 Higashi-Ikebukuro (tel. 5391-5900), with a basement entrance to the left after you disembark from the moving sidewalk. Japan's largest automobile showroom, it boasts five floors of exhibition space. Everything from sports cars and racing cars to family cars and luxury cars are on view, all open so that potential customers can climb inside and fidget with the dials. Be sure to stop by the information desk on the first floor for an English pamphlet. In addition to car models, there are educational programs, including a movie showing the

assembly process (viewers wear 3-D glasses to get the full effect) and a display using holograms to show what goes into making a car. A specially designed theater, free on a first-come first-serve basis, features action films heightened by seats that actually move and machines that emit aromas to match what's happening on the screen. I'm not a big car fan, but even I have fun at Amlux. Everything is free, and the opening hours are Tuesday through Saturday from 11am to 8pm and Sundays and holidays from 10am to 7pm.

Return to the basement and turn left out of Amlux into Sunshine City, which will soon bring you to an information counter. If you wish, ask for directions to the following sights. Otherwise, just continue walking straight through the entire complex, which will bring you to the following attractions in the order presented below. First, in the Sunshine 60 Building, you'll see signs for the:

11. **Observatory** (tel. 3989-3331), with a ticket counter up on the first floor. One of the fastest elevators in the world, traveling at a rate of almost 2,000 feet per minute, whisks visitors to the 60th floor in 35 seconds. Although the Sunshine 60 Building is no longer the country's tallest, it certainly is one of the tallest buildings in this neck of the woods, with a view that is breathtaking. For those who don't suffer from vertigo, there's an even higher open-air platform up a flight of stairs, with diagrams pointing out the city's landmarks. On clear days you can see as far as 60 miles away, including that evasive Mt. Fuji, usually shrouded in a cloak of clouds. A cafeteria serves drinks, ice cream, and snacks, and there's also the ubiquitous souvenir shop. The Observatory is open from 10am to 10:30pm daily (by the way, if you want to forgo the price of the Observatory, take one of the regular slower elevators to the 59th floor Le Trianon Lodge, described in "Take a Break," below).

Past the ticket counter for the Observatory is a digitally controlled dancing fountain, which delights children and parents alike with its changing colors and various patterns. There are also lots of shops here, with more than 200 boutiques selling everything from accessories and fashion to books and fast food. On the 10th floor of the World Import Mart, built as Japan's first general import center, is the complex's most unexpected attraction, the:

12. **International Aquarium** (tel. 3989-3466), which claims to be the world's highest aquarium. It's the unlikely home to more than 20,000 fish and animals, including dolphins, octopus, eels, piranhas, seahorses, sea otters, seals, giant crabs, and rare—and rather weird—species of fish. There are several shows, including performances by sea lions and by an electric eel that gives off an electric charge when provoked. The fish performance takes place every hour, and in my opinion is the highlight of the aquarium, simply for its absurdity (another one of those "only in Japan" things). The aquarium is open Monday through Saturday from 10am to 6pm and Sunday and holidays from 10am to 6:30pm. Admission is charged.

Also on the 10th floor is a planetarium, but since programs are only in Japanese you're better off continuing to the Bunka Kaikan cultural center at the end of the Sunshine City complex, where you'll find the:

13. **Ancient Orient Museum** (tel. 3989-3491) on the seventh floor. Founded with the aim of educating the public about the influences ancient Asian cultures had upon one another, the museum focuses on cultural development through changing displays of pottery, jewelry, ritual objects, reliefs, and statues and other ancient art. Most of the collection stems from the museum's excavations in Syria, though Egyptian, Iranian, Chinese, Japanese, and other ancient cultures are also featured. It's open from 10am to 5pm, closed on Monday. Admission is charged.

There's an entrance to the Higashi-Ikebukuro station in Sunshine City. Alternatively, you can walk back to Ikebukuro Station in about five minutes.

Take a Break   A great place for a snack, coffee, or cocktail is **Le Trianon Lodge** on the 59th floor of the Sunshine 60 Building. Part of the Ikebukuro Prince Hotel, it's open Monday to Saturday from noon to midnight and Sunday and holidays from noon to 11pm; it offers a special buffet daily from noon to 4pm, with fruit, salads, and pastries.

ESSENTIALS &
RECOMMENDED READING

Because much of Tokyo looks monotonously the same when viewed from the inside of a speeding train or taxi, the only way to truly explore the various neighborhoods is on foot. Unfortunately, due to the city's size, its complicated address system, its winding streets, and the language barrier, Tokyo is not an easy city to navigate. With the help of this guide, however, and maps and information supplied by the Tourist Information Center (TIC), you should be able to find your way around the city, seeing most of the major sights and learning about the city's history along the way.

GETTING THERE

For most readers of this book, a trip to Tokyo is likely to begin with an airplane ride across the Pacific. Major carriers flying between the United States and Tokyo include All Nippon Airways, American Airlines, Continental Airlines, Delta Airlines,

Japan Airlines, Korean Air, Northwest Airlines, Malaysia Airlines, Singapore Airlines, Thai Airways International, and United Airlines.

To get a head start on your travel adventure, however, it seems only appropriate to fly Japan's own Japan Airlines (JAL), where you are introduced to Japanese culture as soon as you enter the plane and are greeted by a bow and smile from the flight crew. After the craft leaves the ground, you are handed a steaming towel called *oshibori* with which to refresh yourself. Japan Airlines was the first to introduce the use of oshibori on international flights, a great custom that has since been adopted by other international airlines around the world.

If you're flying first class, JAL's royal treatment begins even before you leave the ground, as you step up to the special first-class check-in counter, where your baggage is loaded into a special container so that it's the first to be unloaded upon arrival in Tokyo. You will also be invited to use the private Sakura Lounge (at major gateways only), a special waiting lounge with free alcoholic drinks, coffee, soda, and snacks. On board the plane you'll have a comfortable, electronically operated seat that reclines to a 60-degree angle; some flights even feature an automatic massage chair that can provide three different styles of massage: *shiatsu* (pressure) massage, a pounding massage, and a rolling type of massage covering the neck, shoulders, and lower back. Some flights also have a personal 5-inch video screen built into the seat armrest, complete with noise-cancelling head phones made especially for JAL by Sony; other flights offer portable videos for private viewing. On some flights, passengers in first and business class can even request video game cassettes, a good way to fight boredom on long flights. In addition to receiving a complimentary toiletry kit and complimentary champagne and other alcoholic beverages, you will be given a choice of five entrees of Western- or Japanese-style cuisine.

Most carriers offer a separate business class, but JAL's Executive Class is probably the largest, with 120 seats. It also has its own check-in counter at the airport, and at the New York and Tokyo airports there's also a special business-class waiting lounge. Other perks include seats that recline 57°; complimentary travel kit; free champagne, cocktails, and wine; and personal videos available upon request. Meals feature both Japanese and Western cuisine.

Arriving by Plane at Narita Airport

The New Tokyo International Airport is located in Narita, about 40 miles from downtown Tokyo, and consists of two terminals, Terminal 1 and 2. Both have banks for money exchange and post offices and are connected to all ground transportation into Tokyo. The Tourist Information Center (TIC), however, is located only in the arrivals lobby of Terminal 2 and is open daily from 9am to 8pm. The TIC offers free maps of Tokyo and sightseeing information, and its staff can direct you to your hotel or inn or even make hotel reservations for you. If you arrive in Terminal 1, you can reach Terminal 2 by taking the shuttle bus from gate 8.

Getting into Town   Everyone grumbles about the Narita airport because it's so far away from Tokyo. In fact, Narita is a different town altogether, with miles of paddies in between. Taking a taxi to Tokyo is prohibitively expensive, costing more than $240 for the one-and-a-half to two-hour ride.

The most popular and convenient way to get from Narita to Tokyo is via the Airport Limousine Bus, which has ticket counters in the arrivals lobbies of both terminals and which deposits passengers at the Tokyo City Air Terminal (TCAT), Tokyo Station, Shinjuku Station and more than 30 major hotels. Buses operate most frequently to TCAT, with the trip taking about 70 to 90 minutes, depending on traffic conditions. Buses depart for hotels approximately every hour; the trip to the Asakusa Prince Hotel in the middle of Tokyo takes almost two hours. Another company that operates buses to more than 20 hotels in Tokyo is the Airport Shuttle Bus, with counters in the arrivals lobbies of both terminals.

You can also reach Tokyo by train, with several options available. Trains depart directly from the airport's two underground stations, called Narita Airport Station (under Terminal 1) and Airport Terminal 2. The JR Narita Express (N'EX) is the fastest way to reach Tokyo, Shinjuku, Ikebukuro, and Yokohama stations, with trains departing every 30 to 60 minutes and the trip to Tokyo Station taking a little less than one hour. All seats are reserved and can be booked in advance through any of JAL's overseas offices or at the airport's basement-level N'EX counter.

An alternative is the privately owned Keisei Skyliner train, which departs from the basements of both terminals and reaches Ueno Station in Tokyo one hour later. Trains depart every 40 minutes or so, and there's a Keisei Skyliner counter in the basements of both terminals.

ORIENTATION/CITY LAYOUT

Tokyo is huge, consisting of 23 wards, known as *ku*. Its business district of Hibiya, for example, is in Chiyoda-ku, while the Ginza is part of Chuo-ku. These two ku are the historic hearts of Tokyo, for it was here that the city had its humble beginnings. Fortunately for visitors, even though Tokyo itself is large, most of Tokyo's attractions, hotels, and most famous restaurants are centrally located, contained within or just outside of a circular commuter railway loop called the Yamanote Line.

The main obstacle in finding your way around Tokyo is that most of its streets don't have names. Imagine what that means in Tokyo—12 million people milling around in a metropolis of nameless streets. Granted, major thoroughfares and some well-known streets in areas like Ginza or Shinjuku have names received after World War II on the insistence of American Occupation forces, but for the most part Tokyo's address system is based on a complicated number scheme that must make the post office's job a nightmare. To make matters worse, most streets in Tokyo aren't straight but zigzag all over the place, a maze apparently left over from olden days when it was designed to confuse any enemies that might attack. Today the streets in Tokyo confuse not only foreign tourists but Tokyo residents themselves.

Among Tokyo's most important thoroughfares that do have names are Meiji-dori, which follows the loop of the Yamanote train line from Ebisu in the south through Shibuya, Harajuku, Shinjuku, and Ikebukuro in the north; Yasukuni-dori and Shinjuku-dori, which cut across the heart of the city from Shinjuku to Chiyoda-ku; and Sotobori-dori, Chuo-dori, Harumi-dori, and Showa-dori, all of which pass through Ginza.

Finding an Address Because most streets are unnamed, Japan has developed a unique postal address system based on geographic entities rather than streets. A typical Tokyo address begins with three numbers, as in the address for the Inakaya restaurant, 7-8-4 Roppongi, Minato-ku 106. Minato-ku is the ward; 106 is the postal code, similar to the U.S. zip code. Within Minato-ku are various districts; in this case the district is Roppongi. Roppongi is further broken down into *chome,* indicated by the first number in the series, in this case 7-chome.

Number 8 refers to a smaller geographical area within the chome, often an entire block, sometimes larger. Although areas 7 and 9 will probably be adjacent to area 8, that is not always the case due to Tokyo's convoluted streets. In addition, houses on one side of the street will almost invariably have a different middle number from houses on the other side. The last number, in this case 4, usually refers to the actual building, although in some rare cases a row of small buildings or residences will have the same last number. And finally, whereas it seems reasonable to assume that next to building 4 will be building 5, even this is not always the case, as buildings were assigned numbers in the order they were constructed, not according to lot location.

Addresses are usually, but not always, posted on buildings, either beside the front door or at one end of the facade. In some cases, the first of the three-number address (the chome) will be written in Japanese characters; the district itself, such as Roppongi, is also likely to be written in Japanese. Thus, in the address for the Inakaya restaurant above, "7" and "Roppongi" may be in Japanese, leaving only "8-4" as decipherable. However, finding even those two numbers is a good bet you've zeroed in on the right building or at least are very close.

Another good place to look for addresses are telephone poles, which carry the first two numbers of the address and the district's name, though often only in Japanese. In recent years, addresses have been added below stop lights at major intersections in some parts of the city.

As you walk around Tokyo, you will notice neighborhood maps posted beside sidewalks giving a breakdown of the number system for the immediate area. The first time I tried to use one, I stopped first one Japanese, then another, and asked them to point to my destination on the map. They both studied the map and pointed out a location; both turned out to be wrong. Not very encouraging, but if you learn how to read these maps, they're invaluable. Although Tokyo's address system might seem rather daunting, it is possible to crack its code—I consider finding addresses in Japan a challenge, akin to finding clues on a treasure map.

Another important source of information is the numerous police boxes, called *koban,* spread throughout the city and identifiable by their gold star and red light. Police staffing these tiny, neighborhood posts know their areas intimately, often have maps of the area, and are very helpful. You should also never hesitate to ask a Japanese the way, but be sure to ask more than one if you're asking directions to all but the most famous attractions. You'll be amazed at the conflicting directions you'll receive. Apparently, the Japanese would rather hazard a guess than leave you standing there. The best thing to do, then, is to ask directions of several Japanese and then follow the majority opinion. You can also duck into a shop and ask someone where a nearby address is, although it has been my experience that employees may not even know the address of their own store.

Street Maps Before setting out on your own, arm yourself with a few maps. Maps are so much a part of life in Tokyo that they're often included as part of a shop or restaurant's advertisement, brochure, or business card, and even appear on private party invitations. A map I find particularly useful is issued free by the Tourist Information Center; it's called **Tourist Map of Tokyo** and includes smaller, detailed maps of several districts (such as Shinjuku) as well as subway and Greater Tokyo train maps. With this map you should be able to locate at least the general vicinity of every walk described in this book. Hotels also sometimes distribute their own maps. In short, never pass up a free map.

GETTING AROUND

By Public Transportation

Since automobiles are a luxury in crowded and expensive Tokyo, you can be sure that the city's public transportation system is efficient in serving the needs of its millions of commuters. Subways and JR commuter trains are the easiest for visitors to use, since destinations are written in English and stations are conveniently located near all the city's major attractions. And since traffic jams are a common occurrence on Tokyo's crowded streets, subways are often the fastest way to zip around the city.

By Subway To get around Tokyo on your own, it's imperative to learn how to ride its subways. Fortunately, Tokyo's subway system is efficient, modern, clean, and easy to use, and all station names are written in English. Subway entrances are identified by a blue S logo. Altogether there are 12 subway lines crisscrossing underneath the city on more than 100 miles of track, some more than 100 feet below ground. There's a subway map on the *Tourist Map of Tokyo* distributed free by the TIC.

Even more information is available in a free publication, "How to Ride Tokyo Subways," also available at the TIC.

Most subways run from about 5am to midnight, though the times of the first and last trains depend on the line, the station, and whether it's a weekday or weekend. Schedules are posted in the stations, and through most of the day trains run every three to five minutes. Avoid taking the subway during the rush hour, from 8 to 9am. The stories you've heard about commuters packed into trains like sardines are all true.

Each subway line is color-coded, which makes transfers easy. The Ginza Line, for example, is orange, which means all its coaches are orange and all signs leading to the Ginza Line platform are also orange.

Before boarding a subway, you must first determine the correct fare and then purchase a ticket from a vending machine. To determine the fare, look at the large subway map above the vending machines, which shows the destinations along each route and the corresponding fares needed to reach them. Unfortunately, destinations are usually written only Japanese, but in recent years, most stations have begun posting a small map listing fares in English (so small, in fact, that you might have to search for it). An alternative is to look at your TIC subway map—it lists stations in both Japanese and English. Once you learn how some Japanese characters look, you may be able to learn how to locate your station and the corresponding fare on the huge subway map above the vending machines.

Once you've determined your fare, you're ready to tackle the vending machine. Insert either coins or a ¥1,000 note, and then punch the button with the price of the ticket you want to buy. Vending machines give change; there are also changing machines for larger yen notes. If you don't want to hassle with coins every time you board the subway, you might consider purchasing a Metro Card, available from a special machine next to the ticket machines. Simply insert it into the special slot of the ticket machine, select your fare, and retrieve the Metro Card along with your ticket. Every time you use the Metro Card, the price of the ticket is deducted from the total value of the card, with the remaining yen amount shown on the vending machine. If you think you're going to be using Tokyo's public transportation system a lot on a particular day, you might consider purchasing a One-Day Open Ticket, which allows unlimited travel on the

Ginza, Marunouchi, Hibiya, Tozai, Chiyoda, Yurakucho, Namboku, and Hanzoman lines. The Tokyo Combination Ticket is a one-day ticket good for use on any subway, streetcar, bus, or JR train in the metropolitan area.

If you can't figure out the fare, ask one of the station attendants for help. An alternative is to simply buy the cheapest ticket available, making up the difference at your destination by going to the "fare adjustment" window and showing the attendant your ticket. In any case, you must validate your subway ticket before boarding the subway by inserting it into a slot at the automated wicket gate. Hold on to your ticket, since you must give it up at the end of your journey by reinserting it into the wicket gate.

Upon exiting the train, you'll find yellow signs outlining the various exits and the sights, buildings, and districts they serve. If you're confused about which exit to take from the station, ask one of the station attendants. Taking the right exit can make a world of difference, especially at Shinjuku Station where there are more than 60 exits from the station.

For information on subway lines, fares, or day tickets, visit one of the English Information Desks at Ginza, Shinjuku, Nihombashi, or Otemachi stations.

By JR Train   In addition to subway lines, there are four electric commuter trains operated by Japan Railways (JR) which run above ground. These are also color-coded, with the green-colored Yamanote Line being the best known and most convenient. It makes a loop around the city, stopping at 29 stations along the way, including Shinjuku, Ueno, Tokyo, and Harajuku stations. Another convenient JR line is the orange-colored Chuo Line, which cuts across the heart of the city between Shinjuku and Tokyo stations.

Buy your ticket from the vending machines the same way you would for the subway. The Orange JR Card operates the same way as the Metro Card, as a pre-paid card good for buying regular tickets. For information on JR commuter trains, call the JR East Infoline at 3423-0111 Monday to Friday from 10am to 6pm.

By Bus   Buses are difficult to use in Tokyo because their destinations are often written only in Japanese and most drivers don't speak English. In this guide, therefore, I have relied exclusively on subways and JR lines as recommended forms of transportation to and from the walking tours in this book. However, during your stay in Tokyo you might find a bus useful for reaching a particular destination. If you're feeling adventurous, board the bus at the front and drop the exact fare into the box next to the driver. If you don't have the exact fare, there's a money machine beside the driver as well. Your change will come out below, minus the fare. To get off the bus, press one of the buttons on the railing near the door or seats.

By Taxi

Hailing a taxi in Tokyo is just like in the movies: You step up to the curb, hold up your arm, and a taxi stops almost immediately. The only time you may have difficulty finding a taxi is when you need one the most—when it's raining or late at night on weekends after all the subways and trains have shut down for the night.

You can hail a taxi from the street or go to a taxi stand. A red light will show above the dashboard if a taxi is free to pick up a passenger; a green light indicates that the taxi is already occupied. Be sure to stand clear of the left back door—it will swing open automatically and will automatically shut once you're in.

Keep in mind that traffic can become so snarled in Tokyo, it's sometimes much faster to take the subway. And unless you're going to a well-known landmark or hotel, it's best to have your destination written out in Japanese, because most taxi drivers do not speak English. But even that may not help. Tokyo is so complicated that often taxi drivers are not familiar with much of it, although they do have detailed maps with them. Don't be surprised if a taxi driver leaps out of the car and dashes into a neighborhood shop—he's asking directions. There are also taxi drivers who may refuse to take you if they don't understand where you're going.

By Car

My advice on driving a car in Tokyo is—don't. Driving a car in Tokyo can make a roller-coaster ride at the local amusement park seem tame stuff. The streets are crowded and unbelievably narrow, street signs are often only in Japanese, and driving is on the left side of the road. Parking spaces can be impossible to find in certain parts of the city, and garages are expensive.

If you're still not convinced, be sure to bring along an international driver's license. There are a dozen major rental-car companies in Tokyo with branch offices spread throughout the city and at Narita airport, including Hertz (tel. 327-9101), Nissan Reservation Center (tel. 3587-4123), Nippon Rent-A-Car Service (tel. 348-7196), and Toyota Rent-A-Car (tel. 3264-2834).

FAST FACTS Tokyo

American Express   The most conveniently located American Express office—and the only one that handles client mail service and emergency card-replacement services—is in Hibiya right across the street from the Tourist Information Center in the Yurakucho Denki Building at 1-7-1 Yurakucho, Chiyoda-ku (tel. 3214-3456). It's open Monday to Friday from 9am to 7pm and Saturday and Sunday from 10am to 5pm; closed on national holidays. The nearest subway station is Hibiya. Another office is in Shinjuku in the Shinjuku Gomeikan Building, 3-3-9 Shinjuku (tel. 3352-1555), open Monday to Saturday from 10am to 6pm, closed on national holidays. The nearest subway station is Shinjuku 3-chome.

Area Code   If you're calling a number in Tokyo from elsewhere in Japan, the area code for Tokyo is 03. If you're calling Tokyo from most countries outside Japan, including from the United States, you should drop the "0" and dial only "3." The country code for Japan is 81.

Bookstores   Maruzen, a well-known bookstore on Chuo-dori at 2-3-10 Nihombashi (tel. 3272-7211), has a large selection of foreign books on its second floor, including all the latest books concerning Japan and things Japanese. It's open Monday through Saturday from 10am to 7pm and on holidays from 10am to 6pm; the nearest station is Nihombashi. Another well-known shop is Kinokuniya Bookstore, 3-17-7 Shinjuku (tel. 3354-0131), located east of Shinjuku Station on Shinjuku-dori. With a wide selection of books and magazines in English on its sixth floor, it's open daily from 10am to 7pm, closed the third Wednesday of the month and on national holidays.

Banks   Banks are open Monday through Friday from 9am to 3pm. You can exchange money at major banks throughout Tokyo, indicated by a sign in English near the front door that says "Authorized Money Exchanger." Generally, banks give better rates of exchange for traveler's checks than for cash.

If you need to exchange money outside bank hours, inquire at one of the larger first-class hotels—most of them will cash traveler's checks or exchange money even if you're not their guest. If you're arriving at the Narita airport, you can exchange money from 9am until the arrival of the last flight.

Business Hours   Stores in Tokyo are generally open from about 10am to 8pm. Often they're closed one day a week, and it's not unusual for almost all shops in a particular neighborhood to be closed on the same day. Some shops, especially those around major train stations and entertainment areas, are open daily and may even stay open until 10pm. Convenience stores, including such chains as Lawson, are open 24 hours.

Department stores are generally open from 10am to 7pm. They close one day a week, but it's different for each store so you can always find several that are open, even on Sunday. In fact, Sundays are big shopping days in Japan.

Museums close their ticket windows 30 minutes before the actual closing time and therefore require that you buy your ticket and enter the museum at least a half hour prior to closing. Similarly, restaurants take their last orders at least 30 minutes before the posted closing time, even earlier for kaiseki restaurants.

Climate   Summer, which begins in June, is heralded by the rainy season, which usually lasts from about mid-June to mid-July in Tokyo and makes umbrellas imperative. When the rain finally stops, it gets unbearably hot and humid through August, with temperatures often in the 80s° F (above 26° C) and humidity almost 90%. The end of August and September is typhoon season, although most storms stay out at sea and vent their fury on land only as thunderstorms.

Autumn, which lasts from September through November, is a pleasant time to visit Tokyo. Winter days are generally clear and cold, rarely below freezing, and usually without heavy snowfall. Spring is ushered in with a magnificent fanfare of plum and cherry blossoms in March and April, with temperatures ranging from about 45° to 65° F (7° to 18° C).

Emergencies   The national emergency numbers are 110 for police and 119 for both ambulance and fire reports. Be sure to speak slowly and precisely.

Holidays   National holidays in Japan are January 1 (New Year's Day), January 15 (Adults' Day), February 11 (National

Foundation Day), March 20 or 21 (Vernal Equinox Day), April 29 (Greenery Day), May 3 (Constitution Memorial Day), May 5 (Children's Day), September 15 (Respect-for-the-Aged Day), September 23 or 24 (Autumn Equinox Day), October 10 (Health and Sports Day), November 3 (Culture Day), November 23 (Labor Thanksgiving Day), and December 23 (Emperor's Birthday). When a national holiday falls on a Sunday, the following Monday becomes a holiday.

Although some businesses close on public holidays, many restaurants and stores remain open. Major museums remain open on public holidays. If a public holiday falls on a Monday (when most museums are usually closed), most museums will remain open but will close the following day instead, on Tuesday. Note that privately owned museums, such as art museums or special-interest museums, generally close on public holidays. To avoid disappointment, call beforehand.

Lost Property If you've forgotten something on a subway, in a taxi, or even a park bench, you need not assume it's gone forever. In fact, if you left something, say, in a telephone booth or in a park, go back and look for it—chances are it will still be there. Otherwise, if you've lost something along a street or outside, go to the nearest koban (local police office). Items found in the neighborhood will stay there for about three days. Afterward, contact the Central Lost and Found Office of the Metropolitan Police Board, 1-9-11 Koraku, Bunkyo-ku (tel. 3841-4151), Monday to Friday from 8:30am to 5pm.

If you've lost something in a taxi or subway, you need to contact the appropriate office. For taxis it's the Taxi Kindaika Center, 7-3-3 Minamisuna, Koto-ku (tel. 3648-0300); for JR trains it's the Lost and Found Section at JR Tokyo Station (tel. 3231-1880) or at JR Ueno Station (tel. 3841-8069). For metropolitan buses, subways, and streetcars, contact the Lost and Found Section of the Tokyo Metropolitan Government, 1-35-15 Hongo, Bunkyo-ku (tel. 3815-7229). And finally, if you've lost something on one of the subways belonging to the Teito Rapid Transit Authority (such as the Ginza, Marunouchi, Yurakucho, Tozai, and Hanzoman lines), call 3834-5577.

Luggage Storage/Lockers Because commuting distances are so great in Tokyo and many office workers and shoppers want to spend the day and evening in the city unencumbered by bags and parcels, there are lockers at all major JR and subway stations in Tokyo, including Shinjuku, Shibuya, Ginza, Roppongi, and countless others. You might find such lockers useful if you're following one of the walking tours and don't want to carry a heavy bag.

Newspapers/Magazines   English-language newspapers published daily in Japan and available at hotel kiosks, bookstores, and some station newsstands are the *Japan Times, Daily Yomiuri, Asahi Evening News,* and the *International Herald Tribune.* In addition, the international editions of both *Time* and *Newsweek* are available. For information on what's going on in Tokyo, pick up a copy of *Tokyo Journal,* a monthly that lists everything from kabuki plays to pop concerts and cinemas.

Restrooms   If you're in need of a restroom, which is always free in Japan, your best bet is at train and subway stations, big hotels, department stores, coffee shops, and fast-food chains like McDonald's. Public toilets, especially those at train stations, are likely to be Japanese style. They're holes in the ground over which you squat facing the end that has a raised hood. Men stand and aim for the hole.

Be sure to carry pocket-size tissue, since toilet paper is rarely provided at public restrooms. Similarly, it's a good idea to carry a handkerchief for drying your hands. To find out if a stall is empty, knock on the door. If it's occupied someone will knock back. Similarly, if you're inside a stall and someone knocks, answer with a knock back or they'll just keep on knocking persistently. If you're in a Japanese-style inn, restaurant, or museum where you must remove your shoes to enter, you'll find special bathroom slippers to wear exclusively inside the restroom area.

Don't be surprised if you go into a restroom and find men's urinals and individual private stalls serving both sexes in the same room. Women are supposed to simply walk right past the urinals without giving them notice.

Taxes   A 3% consumption tax is levied on goods and services, including hotel rates and restaurant meals (the tax is expected to rise to 7% in 1996 or 1997). Visitors from abroad are eligible for a refund of the tax on goods taken out of the country; however, only the larger department stores and specialty shops used to dealing with foreigners seem equipped or willing to follow the procedure. In any case, stores grant a refund only when the total amount of purchases exceeds ¥10,001 for any given store. You can obtain a refund immediately by having the sales clerk fill out a list of your purchases and presenting the list to the tax-exemption counter of that store. You will need to show your passport. Note that no refunds for the consumption tax are given for food, drinks, tobacco, pharmaceuticals, cosmetics, film, or batteries. When you leave Japan at Narita airport, you'll find a counter for the declaration of tax-free articles located just before Customs, where you should leave the receipt you received from the store. Remember, your goods must accompany you out of the country.

As for hotels, a 3% consumption tax will be added to your bill if you stay overnight in lodgings that cost ¥15,000 or less per person. If your lodging costs more than ¥15,000 per person, both a 3% consumption tax and a 3% local tax will be added to your bill. In restaurants, a 3% consumption tax is levied on meals costing ¥7,500 or less, while meals more than ¥7,500 are subject to both a 3% consumption tax and the 3% local tax.

In addition to a tax, a 10% to 15% service charge will be added to your bill in lieu of tipping at most of the fancier restaurants and at many hotels. Thus, the 16% to 21% in tax and service charge can really add up.

Narita airport charges a ¥2,000 departure tax for adults and ¥1,000 for children. There are vending machines that sell departure-tax tickets just past the airline counters, before you enter the Customs area.

Tipping   One of the delights of being in Japan is that there is no tipping, not even of waiters, taxi drivers, or bellhops. Instead of individual tips, a 10% to 15% service charge will be added to your bill at higher-priced hotels and restaurants.

Tourist Information   For foreigners arriving in Tokyo by plane, there's a Tourist Information Center (TIC) in the arrivals lobby of Terminal 2 at Narita airport, open daily from 9am to 8pm.

There's another TIC in the heart of Tokyo at 1-6-6 Yuraku-cho, Chiyoda-ku (tel. 3502-1461), located close to Hibiya and Yurakucho stations and within a 10-minute walk from the Ginza. It's open Monday to Friday from 9am to 5pm and on Saturday from 9am to noon.

In addition, the TIC operates a telephone service from 9am to 5pm every day of the year, called the Travel-Phone. Call 3502-1461 if you're having problems communicating with someone, are lost, or need information on Tokyo.

In addition to the TIC offices above, the Tokyo Metropolitan Government operates three Information Bureaus of Tokyo, where you can obtain information on transportation, shopping, sightseeing, and other aspects of life in Tokyo. One is located at the JR Tokyo Station in a corner of the Yaesu Travel Plaza at the Yaesu Central Exit. It's open Monday to Saturday from 9am to 6pm. The other two are located at Shinjuku Station: at the East Exit, open Monday to Saturday from 9am to 6pm; and at the West Exit, open daily from 8:30am to 6pm.

If you want a quick rundown of what's happening in Tokyo, you can call 3503-2911 for a taped recording in English of what's going on in the city and the vicinity in the way of special exhibitions, performances, festivals, and other events.

For general questions about living in Japan, call the Japan Helpline at 0120-461997, available 24 hours a day.

Finally, be sure to pick up a copy of *Tokyo Journal* for a rundown of what's going on in terms of contemporary and traditional music and theater, exhibitions in museums and galleries, films, and special events. A monthly, it even lists department-store sales, flea markets, apartments for rent, Japanese-language schools, and many other services.

RECOMMENDED READING

General

The definitive work of Japan's history through the ages is provided by Edwin O. Reischauer, a former ambassador to Japan, in *Japan: The Story of a Nation* (Tuttle, 1993). For an overview of Tokyo's recent history, refer to Edward G. Seidensticker's *Low City, High City* (Knopf, 1983), which covers Tokyo's history from 1867 to 1923 when the city rapidly grew from an isolated and ancient shogun's capital into a great modern city, and its sequel, *Tokyo Rising* (Knopf, 1990), which describes the metropolis since the Great Earthquake of 1923 and follows its remarkable development through the postwar years until the end of the 1980s. Arthur Sadler's *The Maker of Modern Japan: The Life of Shogun Tokugawa Ieyasu* (Tuttle, 1987) is a biography of the first Tokugawa shogun, the man responsible for transforming the sleepy town of Edo into the bustling capital of the shogunate government. Paul Waley's *Tokyo: City of Stories* (Weatherhill, 1991) is an informative historical guidebook to Tokyo, with descriptions of Tokyo's major neighborhoods, how they originated and how they developed and changed during the Edo period.

Reischauer's *The Japanese Today* (Tuttle, 1993) offers a unique perspective of Japanese society, including the historical events that have shaped and influenced Japanese behavior and the role of the individual in Japanese society. Other books pertaining to Japanese society and psychology are Kurt Singer's *Mirror, Sword and Jewel: The Geometry of Japanese Life* (Kodansha, 1981) and Chie Nakane's *Japanese Society* (University of California Press, 1970).

A classic describing the Japanese and their culture is the brilliantly written book by Ruth Benedict called *The Chrysanthemum and the Sword* (New American Library, 1967), first published in the 1940s but republished many times since. A more contemporary book is *The Japanese Mind: The Goliath Explained* (Linden Press/Simon & Schuster, 1983), by Robert C. Christopher. I consider this book compulsory reading for anyone traveling to Japan because it describes so accurately the Japanese, the role history has played in developing the Japanese psyche, and problems facing the nation today.

For personal accounts of Tokyo and Japan through the ages, there's no better anthology than Donald Keene's *Travelers of a Hundred Ages: The Japanese as Revealed Through 1,000 Years of Diaries* (Holt, 1989). Written by Japanese from all walks of life, the journals provide fascinating insight into the hidden worlds of imperial courts, Buddhist monasteries, isolated country inns, and more. Lafcadio Hearn, a prolific writer about things Japanese in the late 19th century, describes life in Japan around the turn of the century in *Writings from Japan* (Penguin, 1985), while Isabella Bird, an Englishwoman who traveled alone in Japan in the 1870s, writes a vivid account of what life was like for rural Japanese in *Unbeaten Tracks in Japan* (Virago Press Limited, 1984). For a spirited account of Tokyo during the Meiji era, read *Clara's Diary* (Kodansha, 1979), which begins in 1875 when 15-year-old Clara Whitney arrives in Tokyo with her family and continues for more than a decade with candid observations on everything from shopping on Ginza to national holidays and the demise of traditional Japanese customs in the race to modernization.

For more contemporary experiences of foreigners in Japan, there's the inimitable Dave Barry, who describes his whirlwind trip to the land of the rising sun in the comical *Dave Barry Does Japan* (Random House, 1992). A delightful account of the Japanese and their customs is given by the irrepressible George Mikes in *The Land of the Rising Yen* (Penguin, 1973). Because it was published more than 20 years ago, I doubt you'll be able to find a copy in the United States; it is, however, in major bookstores in Japan and would make light and enjoyable reading during your trip. Rick Kennedy, a longtime resident of Japan, gives a lighthearted view of life in the capital in *Home, Sweet Tokyo: Life in a Weird and Wonderful City* (Kodansha, 1988).

Likewise, the Japan Travel Bureau puts out some nifty pocket-size illustrated booklets on things Japanese, including "A Look into Tokyo," which gives brief descriptions of Tokyo's major neighborhoods, sights, and even festivals, "Eating in Japan," "Martial Arts & Sports in Japan," and "Japanese Family & Culture," which covers everything from marriage in Japan to problems with the mother-in-law and explanations of why dad gets home so late. My favorite, however, is "Salaryman in Japan" (JTB, 1986), which describes the private and working lives of those guys in the look-alike business suits, Japan's army of white-collar workers who receive set salaries. The book is illustrated throughout and includes a picture of the typical salaryman, from his metal-framed, square-rimmed glasses down to his dark-red necktie with diagonal stripes and black leather shoes. The endearing thing about this work is that it was written in complete seriousness, with chapters devoted to life in the salaryman's company, the etiquette of business cards, company trips, the wife of the salaryman, and even the "salaryman blues." Easy to read, it is both entertaining and enlightening.

For advice on Japanese etiquette, refer to *Japanese Etiquette Today: A Guide to Business and Social Customs* (Tuttle, 1994) by James M. Vardaman and Michiko Sasaki Vardaman, which covers everything from bowing and bathing to eating and dining customs, office etiquette, and the complicated art of giving gifts.

For the religions in Japan, two beautifully illustrated books are *Shinto: Japan's Spiritual Roots* (Kodansha, 1980) and *Buddhism: Japan's Cultural Identity* (Kodansha, 1982), both by Stuart D.B. Picken with introductions by Edwin O. Reischauer.

If you find yourself becoming addicted to Japanese food, you might want to invest in a copy of *Japanese Cooking: A Simple Art*

(Kodansha, 1980) by Shizuo Tsuji. Written by the proprietor of one of the largest cooking schools in Japan, this book contains more than 220 recipes, along with information on food history and table etiquette. The history and philosophy of the tea ceremony, beginning with its origins in the 12th century, is given in *The Tea Ceremony* by Sen'o Tanaka (Kodansha, 1983). Another lovely book is *Chanoyu: The Urasenke Tradition of Tea,* edited by Soshitsu Sen XV (John Weatherhill, 1989). It may well be the definitive book on tea and is lavishly illustrated.

Fiction

Reading fiction is certainly one of the most relaxing and fun ways to learn about a country. An overview of classical literature is provided in *Anthology of Japanese Literature* (Grove Press, 1955), edited by Donald Keene. Soseki Natsume, one of Japan's most respected novelists of the Meiji era, writes of Tokyo and its tumultuous time of change in *And Then* (Putnam, 1982), translated by Norma Moore Field, and *Kokoro* (Regnery Gateway Co., 1985), translated by Edwin McClellan.

Because it was also made into a television miniseries, most Westerners are familiar with James Clavell's *Shōgun* (Dell, 1975), a fictional account based on the lives of Englishman William Adams and military leader Ieyasu Tokugawa around 1600. In addition, a vivid history of Japanese woodblock prints from the 17th to 19th century comes alive in the first-person account written by James A. Michener in *The Floating World* (University of Hawaii Press, 1983). Nicholas Bouvier, the Swiss travel writer, mixes personal accounts and art with Japanese history that reads as easy as fiction in his vivid and sensual *The Japanese Chronicles* (Mercury House, 1992).

Other novels written by foreigners include *Ransom* (Vintage, 1985) by Jay McInerney, and *Pictures from the Water Trade* (Harper & Row, 1986) by John D. Morley. Pico Iyer taps into the mysterious juxtaposition of old Japan versus the new in *The Lady and the Monk: Four Seasons in Kyoto* (Alfred A. Knopf, 1991).

INDEX

199